MARY BERRY'S
COUNTRY COOKING

MARY BERRY'S
COUNTRY COOKING

THAMES MACDONALD

Managing Editor
Robin Cross

Art Director
Richard Johnson

Production
John Moulder

Picture Research
Jenny de Gex

Jacket Photograph
Paul Kemp

Food Photography
Rex Bamber

Line Drawings
Joyce Tuhill

Macdonald and Co (Publishers) Ltd
Maxwell House
Worship Street
London EC2A 2EN

ISBN 0 356 09163 5

CONTENTS

INTRODUCTION

Autumn means harvest. It is a time of ripeness
and plenty. It is a time to store up the richness
of the crop, to hold on to some of the summer
sunshine and warm up the winter days ahead.
Game is on the menu, apples are there for the
picking, there is a glut of fresh vegetables and a
chance to get out and about in the countryside
to gather the goodness of the hedgerows and
fields. Pickles, chutneys and preserves are being
made and the rich, warm scents of home baking
fill the kitchen.
I hope that this latest collection of recipes from
my *Afternoon Plus* programme reflects some of
the glories of the season. Its preparation has
been made possible – and enjoyable – by the
help of Clare Blunt. My thanks go to her, as
always, for testing and developing recipes,
typing, answering the telephone, making coffee,
and cheerfully performing miracles.

SALMON
AND TROUT

Just a short time ago salmon and trout were
luxuries, special fish for a special occasion. Now
all this is changing. Thanks to new fish farming
techniques, salmon with all the delicate flavour
of fish caught in the wild is being reared in
Scottish sea lochs, and trout farms are already
flourishing in many parts of the country. Prices
in the shops can only come down. Incidentally,
a visit to the trout farm is an outing for the
whole family, who can pick their individual
fish according to their appetite. Cook the fish as
soon as you get it home, or freeze it. The
simpler the cooking, the better. Grilled trout
served hot needs only melted butter, or serve it
cold with mayonnaise, lemon, cucumber.
Salmon cooks more quickly than you may think,
so never overcook it, it is too valuable to spoil.
And if smoked salmon is too expensive, try
smoked trout instead.

Trout with Almonds

The crispness of the almonds goes well with the fish.

4 trout
A little seasoned flour
3 oz (75 g) butter
2 oz (50 g) halved almonds, skinned
Lemon wedges
Parsley sprigs

Wash the trout under running water to remove any loose blood. If the trout has not been cleaned, make a slit along the belly with a sharp knife and remove the gut; wash very well and then dry on kitchen paper. Coat the fish in flour.

Melt 2 oz (50 g) of the butter in a frying pan and fry the fish for 8 minutes, turning once, over a moderate heat. Carefully lift out of the pan, using a fish slice, and arrange on a warm serving dish.

Add the remaining butter to the pan and when melted add the almonds and fry quickly until golden brown, stirring continuously. Pour this almond and butter mixture over the trout and garnish with lemon wedges and small sprigs of parsley.

Serve at once. Serves 4.

Brandade of Smoked Trout

2 smoked trout about 10 oz (300 g) each
4 oz (100 g) rich cream cheese
2 oz (50 g) butter, melted
Ground black pepper
A little salt
2 tablespoons lemon juice.

FOR TOPPING:
About 1½ oz (40 g) butter, melted
Parsley
Tomato

Slit the trout skin down the back, peel off the skin and discard, then lift the flesh off the bones. Put all the flesh, cream cheese, butter, seasoning and lemon juice in a blender or processor and reduce to a purée. If your machine is small do this in two batches. Check seasoning.

Turn into a 1 pt (600 ml) dish and level. Melt a further 1½ oz (40 g) butter, pour over the top and chill till set. Take out of the refrigerator 1 hour before serving, decorate with parsley and garnish with tomato wedges. Serve with brown bread toast and unsalted butter.

Serves 6–8 as a first course.

Grilled Salmon Steaks with Lemon Hollandaise

Usually the sauce thickens on its own in the goblet of the blender, so there is no need to transfer to a double boiler. As most processors are big, heat is lost when the butter is added, therefore the mixture needs to be heated over a pan of simmering water.

4 salmon steaks about 5 oz (150 g) each
Salt and ground black pepper
A knob of butter for each steak
Lemon juice

SAUCE:
3 egg yolks
1 tablespoon water
2 tablespoons lemon juice
4 oz (100 g) melted butter
Salt and ground black pepper

Season the salmon steaks on both sides, put on the grill rack, dot with butter and a little lemon juice, then grill under a medium grill for 2 to 3 minutes on each side. When cooked the flesh should be pink and opaque. Arrange on a warm serving dish and keep warm while making the sauce.

For the sauce: put the yolks, water and lemon juice in a blender or processor and mix well. Add the hot melted butter in a slow steady stream. Put this mixture in a bowl over a pan of simmering water, stirring continuously until it thickens. Season to taste.

Serves 4.

Brandade of Smoked Trout

Cold Glazed Pink Trout or Salmon

A 4½ to 5 lb (2.0 to 2.3 kg) clean fish will serve 10 people generously and looks wonderful on a buffet table. Cook the fish either in a fish kettle if you have one or in a very large pan or preserving pan. If using a preserving pan make a lid of wide foil to cover it. In fact I like using a pan rather than a fish kettle as you get a beautiful curved fish which sets firmly in shape as you leave it to get cold in the water until the next day.

4½ to 5 lb (2.0 to 2.4 kg) pink trout or
    salmon (weight after cleaning)
2 bay leaves
Peel from one lemon
½ teacup white wine vinegar
12 peppercorns
Few onion rings

GLAZE:
5 tablespoons cold water
1 oz (25 g) powdered gelatine
15 oz can (440 g) consommé
½ cucumber, thinly sliced
Dill, fennel or parsley
2 stuffed green olives

To cook the fish: wash out the belly of the fish and bend into a half circle and fit into a pan or fish kettle which just takes the fish. Use a very thick strip of folded foil to line middle part of the pan and overlap the edge, making sure that the head and tail of the fish are placed within the foil; this helps to lift out the fish later.

Cover with water, add the other ingredients, cover the pan and bring to the boil, boil for two minutes then lift off hob and leave to cool until next day with the lid still on.

Carefully lift the fish from the pan on to a serving dish, using the foil to help you. Then make a sloping cut down both sides of the head and one near the end of the tail (see page 00). Peel off the skin carefully between the head and tail, cool completely. If you have a freezer put the fish in it for an hour to chill the outside flesh. This will help the glaze and cucumber stick quickly. If not, chill the fish in the refrigerator for two hours.

To make the glaze: measure the water into a cup or small bowl, add the gelatine, leave for a few minutes

Cold Glazed Pink Trout

until it is spongy, stand the bowl in a pan of simmering water and leave to dissolve. Remove from the heat and stir the gelatine into the consommé, mix well. If the consommé has come from a cool larder and is set, it should be melted before blending with the gelatine. Leave to become cold but not set. If by chance it should set, melt over a low heat and cool again.

To glaze the fish: remove the eyes and discard. Lightly spoon or brush the glaze over the head and tail of the fish. Then dip each piece of cucumber in the glaze and cover the fish, working from the head. This is not difficult as long as the fish is cold and the jelly sets at once.

Once the fish is covered with cucumber, glaze again; if liked, keep remaining consommé and set in a dish, melting first if it has set. Turn left over consommé on to a piece of wet greaseproof paper and chop with a wet knife. Use to decorate the dish with dill, fennel or a little parsley.

Make "eyes" with the two olives.
Serves 10.

Trout en Croûte

Salmon or Pink Trout en Croûte

A special dish. Make it with a small salmon or a pink trout from a trout farm.

2½ lb (1.1 kg) gutted fresh salmon or
  pink trout
Juice of half a lemon
Salt
Freshly ground black pepper
4 oz (100 g) soft butter
1 teaspoon fresh dill or chives,
  chopped
14 oz (397 g) packet puff pastry
Beaten egg

First bone the fish or ask your fishmonger to do this for you. To do it yourself: take off the head, then fillet the fish by slipping the knife on top of the backbone. Take off the first fillet. Turn the fish over and do the same on the other side and take off the second fillet.

Remove the skin, lay each fillet skin side down on the chopping board and using a sawing action with a sharp knife work along the fillet from the tail, pressing the knife down on to the fish skin at an angle until the skin is removed. Pull out any small bones in the fillets.

Squeeze the juice of the lemon over the fish and season well. Spread half the butter over one fillet, then sprinkle with chopped dill or chives, put the other fillet on top. Spread with the remaining butter.

Roll out the pastry thinly and use to wrap the fish in, sealing the pastry very thoroughly with beaten egg. Keep the fold of the pastry on top. Lift on to a baking tray and decorate with pastry leaves. Glaze with egg.

Chill in the refrigerator until required and bake in the oven at 425 deg.F, 220 deg.C, gas mark 7 for about 30 minutes until golden brown. Serve at once with Fresh Herb Sauce or lemon Hollandaise.

Serves 6.

Barbecue Trout

Small trout cooked in foil over a barbecue on a hot summer's day make a delightful meal.

4 fresh trout
Butter
Foil
Salt
Freshly ground black pepper
4 slices of lemon

Heat the barbecue.

Clean the trout, leaving the heads and tails on. Wipe the fish and dry on kitchen paper.

Cut four good sized squares of foil and butter them. Lay a fish on each piece of foil and season well. Put a small knob of butter inside each fish and lay a slice of lemon on top. Close the foil carefully at the sides and ends to seal the juices in while cooking.

Put on the barbecue and cook over a moderate heat for about 25 minutes, turning once.

Serve the trout from the foil in which it was cooked with all the juices spooned over.

Serves 4.

Kedgeree

Usually this is made with smoked haddock, but if there are any pieces of cooked salmon left, I find this recipe even more delicious.

8 oz (225 g) long grain rice
Salt
2 hard-boiled eggs
About 8 oz (225 g) cooked salmon
4 oz (100 g) butter
Juice of half a lemon
A little paprika pepper
Small sprigs of parsley

Cook the rice in plenty of boiling salted water for about 12 minutes, or as directed on the packet, until tender; rinse well and drain.

Cut a few slices of egg for garnish and roughly chop the remainder. Flake the salmon and remove any bones and pieces of skin.

Melt the butter in a large pan, add the rice, chopped eggs and salmon and heat through very slowly, stirring. Add the lemon juice, salt and a little paprika pepper, taste and check seasoning.

Pile into a warm serving dish and garnish with the slices of egg and sprigs of parsley.

Serves 4.

Salmon Mousse

This is an ideal way of using up the last pieces of a salmon.

½ pint (300 ml) milk
1 bay leaf
Sprig of parsley
Slice of onion
1 oz (25 g) butter
1 oz (25 g) flour
Salt and pepper
½ oz (12.5 g) powdered gelatine
3 tablespoons water
Juice of half a lemon
About 12 oz (350 g) cooked salmon
¼ pint (150 ml) mayonnaise
¼ pint (150 ml) double cream, lightly
   whipped
Cucumber to garnish

Place the milk in a saucepan with the bay leaf, parsley and onion and bring slowly to the boil, then leave to infuse for 10 minutes. Strain.

Melt the butter in a small saucepan, add the flour and cook for a minute. Remove the pan from the heat and blend in the milk, return to the heat and bring to the boil stirring until thickened. Season to taste.

Place gelatine in a small cup with the water and leave to become a sponge. Draw the sauce from the heat and add the gelatine and stir until dissolved.

Flake the salmon, removing the skin and bones and mash with a fork. Put in a bowl and stir in the sauce and lemon juice and mix thoroughly. When cold and starting to thicken, add the mayonnaise and lightly whipped cream. Taste and check seasoning and turn into a 2 pint (1 lt) dish and leave in a cool place to set. Decorate with thin slices of cucumber.

Serves 6.

Cucumber and Dill Mayonnaise

Serve with glazed salmon.

2 egg yolks
1 teaspoon salt
½ level teaspoon made mustard
⅛ level teaspoon white pepper
½ level teaspoon caster sugar
½ pint (300 ml) corn oil
1 tablespoon lemon juice
1 tablespoon wine vinegar
½ cucumber
1 tablespoon fresh chopped dill

Stand the bowl on a damp cloth to prevent it slipping on the table. Put the yolks, mustard, salt, pepper and sugar in a bowl and mix well. Add the oil drop by drop, beating well with a whisk after each addition until the sauce is thick and smooth.

Add the lemon juice and vinegar. Remove the peel and pips from the cucumber and cut into small cubes. Stir into the mayonnaise with the dill just before serving.

Fresh Herb Sauce

Fresh dill is I think preferable to chives for this sauce, but if you haven't any in the garden or can't get it, chives are nearly as good.

3 oz (75 g) butter, melted
Juice of one lemon
Rounded teaspoon flour
½ pint (300 ml) single cream
1 egg
1 teaspoon fresh dill or chives,
   chopped

Put all the ingredients except the dill or chives in the blender or processor, or whisk together until smooth, transfer to a bowl and place over a pan of simmering water. Stir until thick, about 10 minutes.

Season to taste, add the herbs and serve.

MAKING THE MOST OF MEAT

When summer is over, thoughts turn again to
warming, filling dishes, to roasts and casseroles,
meat puddings and stews. Today we all have to
do the best we can with the meat we can afford,
spinning it out with stuffings, dumplings, lots of
vegetables, rice or pasta. The traditional roast
for most of us is an occasional treat, but cheaper
cuts of meat can be transformed into something
special with long, slow cooking and a bit of
imagination about the flavourings. A good stock
is a must for a good stew or casserole. Keep a
supply in the freezer, use stock cubes, too, and
plenty of herbs. Fresh herbs are best and you
can chop them and freeze them in small butter
pots or in ice cubes. Keep the ends of bottles of
wine or cider in small bottles in the fridge for up
to a month and add them to the casserole. Gravy
browning is useful; it is only caramel colouring
but it does brighten up a colourless gravy – and
appearance is important as well as flavour.

Country Lamb

This is a complete meal, with the vegetables cooked underneath the meat.

1 boned shoulder of lamb

STUFFING:
1 oz (25 g) butter
1 onion, chopped
4 oz (100 g) mushroom stalks, chopped
4 oz (100 g) fresh breadcrumbs
2 tablespoons chopped fresh mixed herbs
1 egg, beaten
Salt and freshly ground black pepper

VEGETABLES:
8 oz (225 g) carrots, sliced
2 small onions, quartered
4 sticks celery, sliced
1½ lb (675 g) potatoes, sliced
½ pint (300 ml) stock

Heat the oven to 375 deg.F, 190 deg.C, gas mark 5.

Spread out the boned lamb and trim off any excess fat.

For the stuffing: melt the butter in a small saucepan, add the onion and cook for about 5 minutes until soft and then stir in the mushrooms and cook for 2 to 3 minutes. Remove the pan from the heat and stir in the remaining stuffing ingredients. Spread the stuffing over the meat, press back into shape and seal with skewers.

Place the vegetables in a meat roasting tin, pour over the stock and season well. Put a meat grid on top and lay the lamb on this.

Roast in the oven for about 2 hours or 30 minutes to the lb (450 g). The meat is cooked when the thickest part is pierced with a skewer and the juices run clear.

Lift the lamb off and place on a flat serving dish. Spoon the vegetables into another dish and serve with the meat.

Serves 6.

Rather a Good Cottage Pie

Always a favourite, you can make it in advance and reheat when required.

1 large onion, chopped
4 sticks celery, sliced
1 lb (450 g) raw minced beef
1½ oz (40 g) flour
½ pint (300 ml) beef stock
2 good tablespoons tomato purée
1 teaspoon salt
Freshly ground black pepper
4 oz (100 g) mushroom stalks
1½ lb (675 g) potatoes
A little milk
Butter
2 oz (50 g) grated Cheddar cheese

Place the onion, celery and mince in a saucepan and cook gently for about 5 minutes so that the fat runs out. Stir in the flour and cook for a minute then add the stock, purée, and seasoning and bring to the boil, stirring. Reduce the heat, cover the saucepan and cook gently, stirring occasionally, for about 45 minutes, then stir in the mushroom stalks and cook for a further 10 minutes. Taste and check seasoning and turn into an ovenproof dish.

Meanwhile cook the potatoes in boiling salted water until tender, about 15 minutes. Drain and mash with milk and butter, beat in half the cheese and season to taste. Spread this over the meat.

When required, sprinkle the potato with the remaining cheese and reheat in the oven for about 30 minutes at 400 deg.F, 200 deg.C, gas mark 6. The top will be golden brown and the meat hot through.

Serves 4.

Somerset Pork

Pork, apples and cider go together perfectly in this dish.

4 pork slices or spare rib chops
1 tablespoon oil
2 onions, chopped
1 oz (25 g) flour
½ pint (300 ml) dry cider
Salt
Freshly ground black pepper
2 cooking apples, peeled, cored and cut in chunks
6 tablespoons single cream

Trim any rind from the pork. Heat the oil in a frying pan and fry the pork for 2 to 3 minutes to brown on both sides. Lift out and put on a plate.

Add the onions to the pan and fry, stirring, for about 5 minutes until a pale golden brown. Add the flour and cook for a minute. Stir in the cider and seasoning and bring to the boil. Add the chunks of apples to the sauce, lay the chops on top, cover the pan and cook gently for about 30 minutes or until the pork is tender. If you find the sauce is a little thick, thin down with a little extra cider or stock. The thickness of the sauce will vary with the amount of juice that comes from the apples.

Lift out the slices of pork and place on a serving dish. Taste the sauce and check seasoning and stir in the cream. Once the cream is added do not boil again. Spoon sauce over the chops and serve at once.

Serves 4.

Rutland Lamb

*Taking the bone from the lamb makes
carving easy and each person gets a
good slice with a roll of stuffing in the
middle of it.*

1 leg of lamb
4 slices of ham
2 cloves garlic, crushed
1 teaspoon dried rosemary
Freshly ground black pepper
2 large onions, sliced
1 glass white wine
Salt
Parsley

Bone the leg of lamb. Using a sharp
knife remove the bone, leaving the
shank bone in place, or get the
butcher to do this for you. Heat the

Rutland Lamb

oven to 350 deg.F, 180 deg.C, gas
mark 4.

Spread the slices of ham with the
crushed garlic and sprinkle with some
of the rosemary and pepper. Roll up
and stuff into the lamb in place of the
bone.

Place the onions in a big casserole,
lay the leg of lamb on top. Pour over
the wine and sprinkle with the remaining rosemary and season well.
Cover with a lid or piece of foil and
cook for one hour or 35 minutes to the
lb (450 g) and 35 minutes over. Then
remove the lid and lower the oven
temperature to 325 deg.F, 160 deg.C,
gas mark 3 for the remaining cooking
time. Skim off any fat and serve the
onions and juices with the meat.
Garnish with parsley.

Serves 6 to 8.

Beef in Beer

*There is no stock in this recipe, just a
can of beer to give it a really good rich
flavour.*

1 lb (450 g) stewing steak
1 oz (25 g) dripping
2 onions, sliced
2 sticks celery, sliced
2 carrots, sliced
1 oz (25 g) flour
$15\frac{1}{2}$ oz can (440 ml) light ale
1 teaspoon salt
Freshly ground black pepper
1 bay leaf

Cut the beef into neat one inch
(2.5 cm) cubes. Melt the dripping in
a saucepan and fry the meat quickly
to brown, lift out with a slotted spoon
and put on a plate. Add the vegetables
to the pan and cook for 5 minutes.
Stir in the flour, blend in the beer and
bring to the boil. Return the meat to
the pan with the seasoning and bay
leaf. Cover and simmer for about 2
hours until the meat is tender.

Taste and check seasoning and
remove the bay leaf. Turn into a
warm dish and serve.

Serves 4.

Beef Stew with Dumplings

Dumplings are warming in cold weather. Do not make the mixture too dry or the dumplings will not rise well. Use fresh herbs to give a bright colour.

1 lb (450 g) shin of beef
½ lb (225 g) leg of pork
1 oz (25 g) flour
1 oz (25 g) dripping
2 carrots, sliced
1 parsnip, diced
2 onions, quartered
3 sticks celery, sliced
¾ pint (450 ml) beef stock
Salt and pepper
Bay leaf

HERB DUMPLINGS:
4 oz (100 g) self-raising flour
2 oz (50 g) shredded suet
½ level teaspoon salt
1 tablespoon freshly chopped herbs
6 tablespoons cold water

Cut the meat into one inch (2.5 cm) cubes and toss in the flour. Melt the dripping in a saucepan and fry the meat for 3 to 4 minutes. Stir in any remaining flour. Add the vegetables, stock, seasoning and bay leaf. Bring to the boil, stirring all the time. Cover the saucepan and simmer for about 2 hours or until the meat is tender.

Prepare the dumplings: place the flour in a bowl with the suet, salt and herbs and mix well. Add the water and mix to a soft but not sticky dough. Form into 8 small balls. Place the dumplings on top of the stew and cover and cook for a further 30 minutes.

Turn the stew into a serving dish with the dumplings arranged around the edge and remove the bay leaf.

Serves 4.

Beef in Horseradish Cream

This is a deliciously different way of serving stewing steak and can be prepared well in advance. Only the horseradish cream needs to be added at the last minute.

2 lb (900 g) stewing steak
2 tablespoons dripping
1 large onion, chopped
2 teaspoons curry powder
1 teaspoon ground ginger
1 teaspoon brown sugar
1½ oz (40 g) flour
¾ pint (450 ml) water
2 tablespoons Worcestershire sauce
2 teaspoons salt
¼ teaspoon pepper
3 heaped tablespoons horseradish
  cream
Chopped parsley

Beef in Horseradish Cream

Cut the meat into neat one inch (2.5 cm) cubes, removing any fat.

Heat the dripping in a large saucepan and fry the meat quickly to brown on all sides. Add the onion, curry powder, ginger, sugar and flour and cook for a minute. Stir in the water, Worcestershire sauce and seasoning, cover the saucepan and simmer for 2 hours or until tender.

When ready to serve, stir in the horseradish cream and turn into a warm serving dish. Sprinkle with chopped parsley and serve at once.

Serves 6.

Hambleton Chicken

Large supermarkets now sell minced pork, or you could ask your butcher to mince it for you.

6 chicken breasts, skinned and boned
1 lb (450 g) finely minced pork
3 to 4 eggs, separated
¼ pint (150 ml) double cream
1 teaspoon salt
1 teaspoon sage
2 glasses white wine
1 oz (25 g) butter
1 level tablespoon flour
½ pint (300 ml) chicken stock
¼ pint (150 ml) soured cream
1 teaspoon green peppercorns

Heat the oven to 350 deg.F, 180 deg.C, gas mark 4.

Beat out the chicken breasts slightly and arrange in an ovenproof dish. Put the minced pork in a bowl or a blender or processor and gradually beat in the egg whites and cream, season well and add the sage. Spread over the chicken breasts and pour over the wine.

Bake in the oven for 40 to 45 minutes.

Meanwhile melt the butter in a saucepan, add the flour and cook to a pale straw colour. Add the stock, stirring all the time and simmer until slightly reduced. Add the wine from the chicken.

Blend the egg yolks with the soured cream and add to the sauce, being careful not to let it boil. Season with the crushed peppercorns. Pour the sauce over the chicken and serve at once.

Serves 6.

Roast Duckling with Sage and Onion Stuffing

The classic English way to serve duck.

4 to 5 lb (1.8 to 2.3 kg) oven ready
  duckling
Salt

STUFFING:
2 onions, chopped
1 oz (25 g) butter
4 oz (100 g) fresh white breadcrumbs
1 teaspoon dried sage
½ teaspoon salt
Freshly ground black pepper

Heat the oven to 350 deg.F, 180 deg.C, gas mark 4.

Dry the inside and outside of duck with kitchen paper, prick the skin all over with a fork and sprinkle with salt.

Put the duckling on a grill rack in a shallow baking tin and roast for about 2½ hours without basting, allowing 35 minutes per lb (450 g).

For the stuffing: well butter an 8 inch (20 cm) shallow ovenproof dish. Place the onions in a pan, cover with water and bring to the boil and simmer for 5 minutes, drain well. Return the onions to the pan, add the butter and heat gently until melted, remove from heat and stir in the breadcrumbs, sage and seasoning. Spread in the dish, dot with a little extra butter and bake with the duck for the last 30 minutes of the cooking time. Lift the duck on to a warm dish and serve with the stuffing.

Serves 4.

Veal Fricassé

Stewing or pie veal is usually obtainable from most good butchers.

1 lb (450 g) stewing veal
1 onion, chopped
1 piece of turnip, diced
2 carrots, sliced
1 stick celery, sliced
½ teaspoon mixed herbs
1 clove
4 peppercorns
Small blade of mace
Strip of lemon rind
Salt and pepper
Bacon rolls and chopped parsley to
  garnish

SAUCE:
2 oz (50 g) butter
2 oz (50 g) flour
1 pint veal stock (600 ml)
1 egg yolk
Juice of half a lemon
2 to 3 tablespoons double cream

Cut the meat into neat cubes removing any gristle. Put the meat and vegetables into a large saucepan with the herbs, clove, peppercorns, mace and lemon rind and just cover with hot water. Season well, cover with a lid and simmer gently for 1½ hours or until the meat is tender. Strain off the stock and turn the meat into a warm serving dish, remove the clove, mace and strip of lemon rind.

Melt the butter in a saucepan, add the flour and cook for a minute. Gradually add one pint (600 ml) veal stock, making up to one pint with milk if necessary, stirring continuously. Bring to the boil and cook gently for 2 minutes. Add seasoning to taste then remove from the heat and stir in the egg yolk, lemon juice and cream. Reheat without boiling and pour over the veal and vegetables.

Garnish with bacon rolls and sprinkle with a little chopped parsley.

Serves 4.

FROM THE HEDGEROWS

This is the time of year when there are wonderful things to eat, just for the picking. Go out into the country and you will find the hedgerows full of blackberries, crab apples, sloes and nuts. There are wild mushrooms too in the fields. But do go armed with the right gear. A pound of blackberries can be expensive if the price is a new pair of tights. So wear jeans or trousers. And take a walking stick to help you reach those big juicy berries at the top of the bush. Don't forget something to put your harvest in. Ice cream cartons are better for carrying fruit than a large basket; cartons don't leak and there is no chance for the berries to turn mushy. Deal with the fruit as soon as you get it home, or leave it in the fridge overnight. Peel wild mushrooms, remove stalks, slice and fry in butter. Freeze in small containers for adding to casseroles or soups.

Autumn Jelly

A combination of fruit like this makes a very good jelly.

1 lb (450 g) sloes
1 lb (450 g) elderberries
2 lb (900 g) blackberries
2 lb (900 g) cooking apples, roughly chopped
2 pints (a good lt) water
Granulated sugar

Wash the fruit, place in a large saucepan or preserving pan with the water and simmer gently until all the fruit is tender. Mash well – I use a potato masher to mix the fruit and ensure that it is thoroughly broken up.

Strain overnight in a jelly bag, do not squeeze the bag or the jelly will be cloudy.

Do a pectin test (see below). Measure the juice into the pan and bring to the boil and add 1 lb (450 g) of sugar to each pint (600 ml) of juice. Boil the jelly rapidly until setting point is reached. This will take about 10 minutes. A small amount of jelly dropped on a cold saucer will skin when pushed with the finger.

Remove the jelly from the heat and pour into clean, warm jars. Place waxed circles on top of the jelly and cover with Cellophane or snap-on plastic lids. Leave undisturbed until the jelly has set.

Pectin Test

When the fruit has been simmered and the skins are soft, take a teaspoon of juice, free from skins and pips, and place in a cup; when cold add 3 teaspoons methylated spirit. Shake together and leave for a minute.

If there is plenty of pectin in the fruit a transparent jelly-like lump will form. If the content is moderate the clot of jelly will not be very firm and may be broken into two or three lumps. If there is very little pectin the clot will break into small pieces.

If fruit is low in pectin add a little lemon juice, about 2 tablespoons to each 4 lb (1.8 kg) fruit (the juice from an average lemon). Or add ½ teaspoon citric acid.

Crab Apple Jelly

I make this recipe every year as I am fortunate enough to have a crab apple tree in my garden. The cloves are optional but we like the flavour they give to the jelly.

6 lb (2.7 kg) crab apples
4 pints (2.3 lt) water
1 heaped teaspoon cloves, optional
Juice of one lemon or at least 4 tablespoons lemon juice
Granulated sugar

Wash the crabs and remove all the leaves and stalks and cut out any parts that may be bruised. Put them in a preserving pan with the water, cloves and lemon juice. Bring to the boil and simmer for about 20 minutes or until the crab apples are soft. Mash well with a potato masher, remove from the heat and leave to cool for about 30 minutes. Turn mixture into a jelly bag and leave to strain overnight. I always find that this stage is easier with another pair of hands to help hold the bag!

Next day measure the juice from the jelly bag. Do not squeeze the bag or the jelly will be cloudy. To each pint of juice (600 ml) allow 1 lb (450 g) of granulated sugar. Place both in the preserving pan and heat very gently, stirring until the sugar has dissolved. Then boil fairly quickly for about 10 minutes or until setting point is reached. This is when a small amount dropped on to a cold saucer will skin when pushed with a finger. Remove the jelly from the heat and pour into clean, warm jars. Cover and seal.

Makes about 8 to 9 lb (3.6 to 4.1 kg).

Mint Jelly

Make this jelly with the first of the apples, so that the mint is still fresh with a good flavour.

3 lb (1.4 kg) cooking apples
1 large lemon
1½ pints (900 ml) boiling water
Granulated sugar
1 bunch of young mint
Green colouring

Wipe the apples, then slice with the lemon, including the peel, core and pips. Put in a saucepan with the water, cover and simmer for about 20 minutes or until apples are soft. Mash the apples well and strain through a jelly bag overnight. Measure the juice, which will give about 2 pints (900 ml). For each pint allow 1 lb (450 g) granulated sugar.

Place the sugar and apple juice in a saucepan and heat through until the sugar has dissolved.

Very finely chop the small tender mint leaves and tie the remainder in a bunch with a piece of string and lower into the juice, securing one end of the string to the handle of the pan.

Bring the apple juice to the boil, and boil rapidly until setting point is reached. This is when a small amount dropped on to a cold saucer will form a skin when pushed with a finger.

Lift out the bunch of mint leaves and discard. Add a little green colouring to the jelly and stir in the chopped mint. Leave the jelly to stand for about 5 minutes before potting, so that it will thicken slightly and the mint will be evenly suspended rather than floating on the top.

Pot into small warm jars, cover with a wax disc and screw-top lids or Cellophane paper.

Makes about 3½ lb (1.5 kg).

Loganberry or Blackberry Ice Cream

The fruit for this ice cream is raw and gives a delightful colour to the ice cream.

1 lb (450 g) loganberries or
   blackberries
4 eggs, separated
4 oz (100 g) caster sugar
½ pint (300 ml) whipping cream

Purée fruit in blender or processor then sieve out the pips. Whisk the yolks in a small bowl until blended. In a larger bowl whisk the egg whites with a hand rotary or electric whisk until stiff. Then whisk in the sugar a teaspoon at a time. The whites will get stiffer and stiffer as the sugar is added. Blend in the egg yolks until no streaks of colour remain. Whisk the cream until it forms soft peaks and fold into the mixture with the fruit purée.

Turn into a shallow 2½ pint (1.41 lt) container, cover, label and freeze until frozen solid. Leave to thaw at room temperature for 5 minutes then serve in scoops in small glasses or dishes with sweet biscuits.
Serves 8.

Sloe Gin

Sloes are the fruit of the blackthorn and are like very small damsons with a blue bloom. A very bitter fruit is best for gin or fruit jellies.

Wash the sloes, remove the stalks and snip each sloe with scissors or a sharp knife.

Take a clean empty gin bottle, or similar, and fill two thirds with snipped sloes. To each bottle add 8 to 10 oz (225 to 275 g) caster sugar and then fill the bottle up with gin. Put the lid on and shake the bottle very well.

Put on one side for at least two months before using, shaking the bottle about twice a week. In theory you should not drink it for at least six months.

Serve in small glasses as an after dinner drink.

After six months, strain the gin from the sloes and discard them.

Loganberry Ice Cream

Apple and Pepper Relish

Windfall apples are perfect for this recipe as the fruit is prepared first and weighed afterwards.

2 lb (900 g) cooking apples, peeled
   and cored and weighed after
   preparation
2 onions, quartered
6 tablespoons malt vinegar
12 oz (350 g) demerara sugar
1 rounded teaspoon mustard powder
Grated rind and juice of one lemon
2 bay leaves
6 oz (175 g) sultanas
1 level tablespoon salt
½ level teaspoon mild chilli powder
2 level teaspoons ground ginger
2 cloves garlic, crushed

Mince the apples and onions and place in a thick based saucepan with the vinegar, sugar, mustard, lemon rind and juice. Simmer for 20 minutes and then add the remaining ingredients, stir well.

Bring to the boil and reduce the heat and simmer, stirring occasionally until the mixture is fairly thick with a chutney consistency. This will take about 45 minutes.

Remove the bay leaves and pot the relish in clean, warm jars. Seal with plastic or vinegar proof lids. Label.

Makes a good 3 lb (1.4 kg).

Green Tomato Chutney

Make this chutney with the last of the home grown tomatoes that somehow never seem to ripen.

3 lb (1.3 kg) green tomatoes, skinned and sliced
1 red pepper, seeded and chopped
12 oz (350 g) onions, sliced
12 oz (350 g) cooking apples, weighed when peeled, cored and chopped
6 oz (175 g) raisins
¾ oz (19 g) salt
One inch (20 cm) pieces, peeled root ginger
A little cayenne pepper
12 oz (350 g) brown sugar
1 pint (600 ml) malt vinegar

Place all the ingredients in a preserving pan and simmer gently, stirring occasionally, for 2 to 3 hours. The mixture will be of a thick consistency and all the liquid absorbed.
Remove the piece of root ginger and pot in clean warm jars. Seal with plastic or vinegar proof lids.
Makes about 5 lb (2.3 kg).

Garlic Mushrooms

Choose only the smallest white button mushrooms for this recipe.

8 oz (225 g) small button mushrooms
2 to 3 oz (50 to 75 g) butter
1 clove garlic, crushed
Salt
Freshly ground black pepper
Chopped parsley

Wipe the mushrooms and trim the ends of the stalks.
Melt the butter in a frying pan, add the garlic and mix well.
Put the mushrooms in the pan and cook gently for 5 minutes. Season well and sprinkle in the parsley. Turn into a warm serving dish, pouring over any butter and herbs left in the pan.
Serves 4.

Chutney in the Raw

In this recipe the vegetables are fairly small and just cooked for 5 minutes to keep them crisp.

1 marrow, peeled, seeded and finely diced
1 cucumber, finely diced
3 carrots, grated
3 onions, grated
1 cauliflower, broken into tiny pieces
10 oz (275 g) salt
5 pints (2.8 lt) water

SAUCE:
3 oz (75 g) flour
½ oz (12.5 g) curry powder
½ oz (12.5 g) turmeric
1½ oz (40 g) mustard powder
2 pints (a good litre) malt vinegar
1¼ lb (550 g) granulated sugar

Place all the prepared vegetables in a large bowl or plastic bucket and add the salt and water and leave to soak for 24 hours.
Next day rinse the vegetables and drain very thoroughly.
Put the flour and spices in a preserving pan and gradually blend in the vinegar to make a smooth paste. Add the sugar and bring to the boil, stirring until thickened.
Add the vegetables, bring back to the boil and boil for 5 minutes. Remove from the heat and pot in clean warm jars and seal with plastic or vinegar proof lids.
Makes about 9 lb (4.0 kg).

Blackberry and Apple Trifle

1 packet of 8 trifle sponges
Bramble jelly
¼ pint (150 ml) cider
8 oz (225 g) cooking apples, after peeling and coring
8 oz (225 g) blackberries, reserving a few well shaped ones for decoration
1 tablespoon sugar
½ pint (300 ml) custard, see below
¼ pint (150 ml) whipping cream, whipped until stiff

Split the sponges, spread with bramble jelly and sandwich them together. Cut each sponge into 6 small squares and line the bottom of a 9 inch shallow glass bowl. Pour the cider over the cut up sponges. Peel, core and slice the apples and put with the blackberries and sugar into a saucepan and simmer for about 5 minutes until soft. Cool and spread on top of the sponges.

CUSTARD:
3 egg yolks
1 oz (25 g) caster sugar
1 heaped teaspoon cornflour
½ pint (300 ml) milk

Mix together the egg yolks, sugar and cornflour. Warm the milk in a pan until hand-hot and pour on to the egg yolks, stirring constantly. Return the mixture to the saucepan and cook gently, stirring until it thickens. Do not allow it to boil or the custard will curdle.
Cool and then pour on top of the blackberry and apple. Allow to set completely and then top with the whipped cream and decorate with the reserved blackberries.
Serves 6 to 8.

Blackberry and Apple Trifle

APPLES AND PEARS

In a good apple year there is more than enough for everyone and then the problem is to know what to do with the glut. The family may tire of apple pie every Sunday, the cook may tire of making it. So if you have your own apple trees, if friends inundate you with fruit, or even if you are tempted by the reasonable price in the greengrocer's, don't waste your apples. Store them for the months ahead. But store only perfect fruit. Wrap them individually in newspaper and keep them, not touching each other, in a frost-free shed or garage, on shelves or on greengrocer's trays in the larder. They freeze well, as purée for sauce or cooked to use in pies or crumbles. Many recipes need only windfalls, so use up the damaged fruit and store the best. As you peel, toss the slices in lemon juice to stop them discolouring, or put them in salt water (rinse well before using). Pears can be treated in the same way; they freeze well in a honey syrup.

French Apple Flan

PASTRY:

6 oz (175 g) plain flour
2 oz (50 g) butter
2 oz (50 g) lard
1 egg yolk
½ oz (12.5 g) caster sugar
2 teaspoons cold water

FILLING:

4 oz (100 g) sugar
3 level tablespoons cornflour
¾ pint (450 ml) milk
4 egg yolks
1 teaspoon vanilla essence

TOPPING:

1½ lb (675 g) cooking apples, sliced
Butter
Sugar

First make the pastry. Measure the flour into a bowl, add the fats cut into small pieces and rub in with the fingertips. When the mixture resembles fine breadcrumbs, mix in the egg yolk, sugar and water and bind together. Roll out the pastry on a floured board and line a 9 inch (22.5 cm) flan tin. Chill for 30 minutes.

Heat the oven to 425 deg.F, 220 deg.C, gas mark 7, with a thick baking sheet in it. Line the flan with grease-proof paper and weigh down with baking beans and bake blind for 15 minutes. Remove the paper and beans after 10 minutes and then return the flan to the oven to dry out.

Meanwhile prepare the filling. Put the sugar and cornflour in a saucepan and blend with a little of the milk. Add the remaining milk and bring to the boil, stirring all the time, until the mixture thickens, cook for a minute.

Remove the pan from the heat and beat in the egg yolks one at a time. Return the pan to the heat and cook very gently for 5 minutes, stirring continuously, but do not allow to boil. Remove from the heat and leave to cool. Add vanilla essence, and pour into the pastry shell.

Arrange the apple slices on a baking sheet, brush with melted butter and sprinkle with a little sugar and brown under the grill. Carefully lift off and arrange over the cream filling in over-lapping circles.

Serve warm or cold (6 to 8).

Summer Pudding

This delicious pudding can be made from any combination of fruits in summer and is always best made a day in advance.

2 lb (900 g) mixed soft fruits, to include:
8 oz (225 g) blackcurrants
8 oz (225 g) raspberries
8 oz (225 g) peeled, cored and sliced apples
8 oz (225 g) black cherries, stoned
4 oz (100 g) granulated sugar
6 tablespoons water
12 slices white bread

Place all the fruit in a saucepan with the sugar and water and simmer gently until tender, this will take about 5 minutes. Leave to cool. Remove the crusts from the bread and line a 2 pint (1 lt) bowl with the bread, or use a round fairly shallow dish. Keep one or two slices of bread for the top.

Turn the fruit into the bowl or dish, place the slice of bread on the top and bend over the tops of the sliced bread at the sides towards the centre. Put a saucer on top, pressing down well until the juices rise, to soak each slice of bread. Leave overnight in the refrigerator.

Turn out just before serving and serve with lots of cream.

Serves 4 to 6.

Roast Pork with Kidneys and Glazed Apples

An easy to carve roast good for entertaining. Fry the apples at the last moment before serving.

3½ lb (1.5 kg) joint loin pork, boned, crackling left on
2 pork kidneys
8 oz (225 g) pork sausagemeat
Tablespoon chopped parsley
Teaspoon rubbed dried sage
Salt
Ground black pepper
Little oil

GLAZED APPLES:

4 Cox's apples
2 tablespoons demerara sugar
1 oz butter

Get the butcher to bone the loin for you, use the bones for stock – they will weigh about 12 oz. Also have the crackling finely scored.

Remove skin from the kidneys and snip out the core with sharp scissors or a knife. Mix sausagemeat with herbs and seasoning. Turn the joint skin side down on the board. With a very sharp knife remove any pieces of white tough skin where the rib bones were, season lightly and spread with sausagemeat, lay kidneys side by side lengthways.

Secure the joint with about 3 skewers, or with string. Turn over on a piece of foil, lift into roasting tin with the crackling uppermost. Rub with oil, sprinkle with salt and roast at 350 deg.F, 180 deg.C, gas mark 4 for about 2 hours until the crackling is crisp and when the meat is prodded with a fine skewer the juices that run out are clear.

While the joint is cooking prepare the apples. Core apples, leaving the skin on, cut in thickish slices to make rings, toss in demerara sugar then brown quickly in butter in a frying pan. Serve with the pork and make a thin gravy from the juices from the meat.

Serves 6 to 8.

Roast Pork with Kidneys and Glazed Apples

Apple Dumplings

A schoolboy favourite, filling and warming in winter. Serve with custard.

PASTRY:
10 oz (275 g) plain flour
2½ oz (62.5 g) margarine
2½ oz (62.5 g) lard
About 3 tablespoons cold water
4 medium-sized cooking apples, peeled and cored
1½ oz (40 g) light soft brown sugar
1½ oz (40 g) mixed dried fruit
A good pinch mixed spice
Milk
Granulated sugar

Heat the oven to 400 deg.F, 200 deg.C, gas mark 6.

Place the flour in a bowl, add the fats cut in small pieces and rub in with the fingertips until the mixture resembles fine breadcrumbs, add sufficient cold water to mix to a firm dough. Roll out the pastry on a floured surface into four 7 inch (17.5 cm) squares.

Put an apple in the centre of each pastry circle. Mix the sugar, fruit and spice together and use to fill the centre of each apple.

Bring the edges of the pastry together over the apples and, trimming neatly if necessary, press to a smooth shape. Place on a lightly greased baking tray with the sealed edges underneath. Make a hole in the centre top of each dumpling. Roll out any pastry trimmings and use to make leaves and decorate the dumplings.

Brush with milk and bake in the oven for about 35 to 40 minutes, until the pastry is lightly browned. Sprinkle with a little granulated sugar if liked and serve hot.

Serves 4.

Chocolate and Pear Pancakes

These pancakes may be made in advance and then reheated under foil in a cool oven for a short while.

BATTER:
4 oz (100 g) plain flour
1 level tablespoon caster sugar
1 level tablespoon chocolate powder
2 eggs
½ pint (300 ml) milk or milk and water mixed
Oil

FILLING:
½ pint (300 ml) whipping cream
1 lb (450 g) poached sliced pears (see next recipe)

For the pancakes: measure the flour, sugar and chocolate powder into a bowl and make a well in the centre. Add the eggs and gradually beat in the milk, or milk and water, using a small whisk, until the mixture is smooth.

Heat a little oil in an 8 inch (20 cm) frying pan. When hot pour off any excess fat and then spoon two tablespoons of the batter into the pan so that it spreads evenly over the base. Cook for about one minute and then turn over with a palette knife and cook on the other side for about one minute. Slip the pancake out of the pan and keep warm while making the remaining pancakes. This batter will make about 8.

For the filling, whisk the cream until thick and then fold in the pear slices. Place about 2 tablespoons of this filling on each pancake and roll up, place on a serving dish and sprinkle with caster sugar. Serve at once.

For a special treat mix a little finely grated chocolate with the sugar and sprinkle over the pancakes.

Serves 4.

To Poach Pears

Use this simple way of poaching cooking pears. They can be used in a variety of dishes, or just served in the syrup in which they were cooked.

¼ pint (150 ml) water
2 oz (50 g) granulated sugar
1 lb (450 g) cooking pears

Place the water and sugar in a shallow pan and heat gently until the sugar has dissolved.

Peel, quarter and core the pears and cut each quarter in 3 or 4 slices, depending on the size of the pears.

Lay the slices in the syrup and poach gently for about 8 to 10 minutes; the time will vary with the type and ripeness of pears, so keep an eye on them and adjust the time accordingly. Turn into a dish and leave to cool. Use as required.

Pears in Cream

This needs to be done at the last moment or it can be left to cook while eating the main course.

4 pears
1 oz (25 g) butter
¼ pint (150 ml) double cream
A little light soft brown sugar

Heat the oven to 350 deg.F, 180 deg.C, gas mark 4.

Peel, core and neatly slice the pears.

Heat the butter in a frying pan and fry the pears for about 10 minutes or until just tender, without browning. Turn into four individual ovenproof dishes. Pour over the cream and bake in the oven for about 15 minutes, when the cream will have thickened slightly.

Remove from the oven, sprinkle with light soft brown sugar and serve at once.

Serves 4.

Pears in Red Wine

Poaching the pears in red wine gives them a pale pink colour. Serve with plenty of cream.

$\frac{1}{4}$ pint (150 ml) red wine
$\frac{1}{4}$ pint (150 ml) water
2 oz (50 g) granulated sugar
4 good sized pears

Put the wine, water and sugar in a shallow pan and heat gently until the sugar has dissolved.

Peel the pears and cut in half lengthwise and scoop out the core with a teaspoon. Lay the pears in a single layer, cut side down, in the pan and poach gently until tender. This will take about 15 minutes, but maybe a little longer if the pears are very hard.

Lift the pears out with a slotted spoon and place in a serving dish. Boil the wine syrup rapidly for 2 to 3 minutes until it has reduced slightly then pour over the pears and leave to cool.

Serves 4.

Apple and Almond Cake

This is best served warm with whipped cream. It freezes well. Once thawed, reheat in the oven until warm. Serve as a dessert or at tea time.

5 oz (150 g) soft margarine
2 large eggs
8 oz (225 g) caster sugar
1 teaspoon almond essence
8 oz (225 g) self-raising flour
1½ level teaspoons baking powder
12 oz (350 g) cooking apples (weight after peeling, coring and slicing)
1 oz (25 g) flaked almonds

Heat the oven to 325 deg.F, 160 deg.C, gas mark 3. Grease an 8 inch (20 cm) loose bottomed tin.

Place all the ingredients except the apples and flaked almonds in a bowl and beat well or use a blender or processor.

Spread half the mixture in the bottom of the tin, and cover this with the sliced apples. Put blobs of the rest of the mixture on top of the apples. Sprinkle with flaked almonds and bake in oven for about 1½ hours until evenly pale brown and shrinking away from the sides of the tin.

Honeydew Minted Pears

A divine combination for a first course, essential that it is served very cold. When small whole Ogen or Galia melons are available you can serve this pear and tomato mixture in melon halves.

1 large honeydew melon, chilled in refrigerator
2 ripe pears
Tablespoon lemon juice
3 firm tomatoes, skinned, halved and pipped
Tablespoon fresh chopped mint
6 sprigs mint

Apple and Almond Cake

FRENCH DRESSING:
¼ teaspoon dry mustard
4 teaspoons sugar
2 tablespoons wine vinegar
4 tablespoons corn oil
Salt
Ground black pepper

Cut melon in half, remove pips. Cut into six wedges, remove flesh from the skins and dice it, keep the 6 skins. Peel pears, core, dice and toss in lemon juice in bowl. Cut tomato flesh in strips, add to the pears with the melon.

Mix mustard, sugar and vinegar together, stir in oil and seasoning, add to the fruit with chopped mint. Chill in refrigerator for 6 hours. Just before serving put melon skins on 6 individual plates, top with melon mixture and decorate with sprig of mint.

Serves 6.

Spiced Pippins

Serve with roast pork or sliced cold meats.

⅛ pint white wine or cider vinegar
2 tablespoons honey
4 Cox's orange pippins
I teaspoon whole allspice
Sprig of fresh rosemary

Boil the vinegar with the honey for a few minutes. Peel, core and slice the apples into eighths. Add to the vinegar with the allspice and simmer gently for 15 minutes, or until transparent. Leave to cool, then pour gently into a 12 oz (350 g) jar, carefully arranging the sprig of rosemary up the side of the jar. Screw down tightly.

Makes one 12 oz (350 g) jar.

Lemon and Pear Meringues

Pears and lemons make a lovely combination.

PASTRY:
6 oz (175 g) plain flour
1½ oz (40 g) margarine
1½ oz (40 g) lard
About 2 tablespoons cold water

FILLING:
2 large lemons
1½ oz (40 g) cornflour
3 oz (75 g) caster sugar
Knob of butter
½ pint (300 ml) water
3 egg yolks
1 lb (450 g) poached pears (see page 30), drained

MERINGUE:
3 egg whites
4 oz (100 g) caster sugar

Measure the flour into a bowl, add the fats cut in small pieces and rub in with the fingertips until the mixture resembles fine breadcrumbs. Add sufficient cold water to mix to a firm dough. Roll out the pastry on a floured surface and line a 9 inch (22.5 cm) flan tin. Chill for 10 minutes.

Heat the oven to 425 deg.F, 220 deg.C, gas mark 7 with a thick baking sheet in it. Line the flan tin with greaseproof paper and baking beans and bake blind for 10 minutes, then remove the baking beans and paper and return to the oven for a further 5 minutes to dry the pastry.

Meanwhile make the filling: grate the rind and squeeze the juice from the lemons. Put the cornflour in a saucepan with the lemon rind and juice and blend to a smooth paste. Add the sugar, knob of butter and water and place over a moderate heat and bring to the boil, stirring until the mixture has thickened. Simmer for 2 minutes.

Remove the pan from the heat and beat in the egg yolks and return to the heat for a moment to thicken the sauce, cool slightly, stir in the pears and turn into the pastry case.

For the meringue: whisk the egg whites with an electric or rotary whisk until they form stiff peaks and add the sugar a teaspoon at a time, whisking well.

Spoon over the filling, taking care to spread the meringue out to the edge of the pastry.

Reduce the oven temperature to 325 deg.F, 160 deg.C, gas mark 3 for about 15 to 20 minutes until the meringue is tinged a pale golden brown.

Serve the pie either warm or cold. Serves 6.

Spiced Pippins

GARDEN FRESH VEGETABLES

Now is the time when the garden is at its most productive, when prices are low in the shops and when you have almost more vegetables than you know what to do with. It is sensible then to eat what you can now and freeze the rest to see you through till next year. Harvest your garden vegetables before they grow too big. Young runner beans, peas, marrows and courgettes need the minimum of cooking, in not too much water, to preserve their tender crispness. A good general rule is to cook green vegetables in an uncovered pan, root vegetables with the lid on. Serve a combination of different vegetables – a few peas mixed with courgettes, for example – and experiment with different ways with potatoes – layer them in a dish with onions, add stock and cook in the oven under the roast or above the casserole. Cheese and vegetable dishes, spinach quiche or cauliflower cheese, perhaps, are welcome for lunch or supper and are economical too.

Mixed Vegetables with Cheese Sauce

This is an ideal vegetable dish to prepare the day before. It goes well with any meat.

1 lb (450 g) potatoes
2 tablespoons milk
Knob of butter
Salt
1 lb (450 g) carrots, sliced
8 oz (225 g) peas
A small cauliflower

SAUCE:
1½ oz (40 g) butter
1½ oz (40 g) flour
¾ pint (450 ml) milk
2 tablespoons grated cheese
Salt and pepper

Peel the potatoes and cook in boiling salted water until tender. Mash with the milk and butter and season to taste.

Cook the carrots in boiling salted water until tender and cook the peas. Break the cauliflower into florets and trim away any hard stalk. Cook in boiling salted water until tender.

For the sauce: measure the butter into a small pan, add the flour and cook for a minute. Blend in the milk and bring to the boil, stirring until the sauce has thickened, and cook for 2 minutes. Add the cheese and season well.

Drain the cauliflower and arrange around the edge of an ovenproof dish and fill the centre with the peas and carrots mixed together. Pour the cheese sauce over the vegetables.

Using a fork, arrange the mashed potato around the edge of the dish covering the cauliflower.

When required, put in the oven at 375 deg.F, 190 deg.C, gas mark 5 for about 25 minutes or until hot through and golden brown.

Serves 6.

Ratatouille

A lovely combination of vegetables that comes from the south of France. If you have a glut of tomatoes in the garden this is an ideal way to use them.

4 tablespoons oil
2 onions, sliced
2 aubergines, sliced
2 green peppers, seeded and sliced
2 cloves garlic, crushed
A little fresh basil
2 beefsteak tomatoes or 1 lb (450 g) tomatoes
Salt
Freshly ground black pepper

Heat the oil in a large thick frying pan and add the onions, aubergines, green peppers, garlic and basil and fry for 5 minutes, stirring constantly. Cover the pan, reduce the heat and cook gently for about 20 minutes, stirring occasionally.

Place tomatoes in a bowl, cover with boiling water and leave to stand for 10 seconds, then drain and peel off the skins. Quarter, remove the seeds and roughly chop. Add to the pan with plenty of salt and black pepper and cook without the lid for about 5 minutes until the aubergines are tender and the tomatoes are soft but still hold their shape.

Serves 4 to 6.

Basil Potatoes

These go very happily with Rutland Lamb (p. 17).

2 lb (900 g) small potatoes, peeled
2 oz (50 g) butter
1 oz (25 g) flour
½ pint (300 ml) milk
¼ pint (150 ml) single cream
2 cloves garlic, crushed
Salt and pepper
1 tablespoon fresh chopped basil
Chopped parsley

Heat the oven to 350 deg.F, 180 deg.C, gas mark 4.

Cut the potatoes in thick slices, cook in boiling salted water for 3 minutes and then drain.

Make a rich white sauce: melt the butter in a saucepan, add the flour and cook for a minute. Remove the pan from the heat and stir in the milk. Return to the heat and bring to the boil, stirring. Blend in the cream, garlic and seasoning. Add the potatoes and then turn into the casserole.

Cook in the oven for about one hour, the sauce will be partly absorbed. Stir in the herbs and then turn into a serving dish.

Serves 6 to 8.

Fried Courgettes

Courgettes are best if served very simply and this is one of my favourite ways of cooking them.

1 lb (450 g) courgettes
2 oz (50 g) butter
Salt
Freshly ground black pepper
One tablespoon fresh chopped mixed herbs

Wash the courgettes, top and tail and cut in ¼ inch (60 cm) slices. Melt the butter in a frying pan and add the courgettes with seasoning and fry over a moderate heat, turning frequently for about 15 minutes until the courgettes are soft and a pale golden brown.

Sprinkle over the herbs and turn the courgettes into a warm dish with any butter still remaining in the pan.

Serves 4.

Fresh Tomato Soup

Sometimes fresh tomato soup does not have a very good colour, so if necessary add a little extra tomato purée.

2 oz (50 g) butter
2 onions, chopped
2 oz (50 g) flour
1½ pints (900 ml) chicken stock
2 lb (900 g) tomatoes, roughly
    chopped
Salt
Freshly ground black pepper
1 bay leaf
A little tomato purée (optional)
Mint to garnish

Melt the butter in a large saucepan, add the onions and cook for 5 minutes until golden brown, then stir in the flour and cook for a minute. Add the stock and bring to the boil, stirring until thickened. Now add the tomatoes, seasoning and bay leaf, bring back to the boil, then reduce the heat, cover the saucepan and simmer gently for 30 minutes.

Sieve the soup into a large bowl.

Rinse out the saucepan, return the soup to it and reheat, adding a little purée if necessary. Taste and check seasoning and serve hot. Garnish with chopped mint.

Serves 6.

Runner Beans with Bacon

For a change try serving runner beans like this – or you could use whole French beans.

1 lb (450 g) runner beans
1 oz (25 g) butter
1 onion, finely chopped
4 rashers streaky bacon, cut in strips

Top and tail the beans and slice them. Cook in boiling salted water for 8 to 10 minutes, until tender, then drain thoroughly.

While the beans are cooking, melt the butter in a saucepan, add the onion and bacon and fry for 5 minutes until the onion is golden brown and the bacon crisp and the fat has run out. Add the beans to this mixture and toss until well blended. Turn into a warm serving dish.

Serves 4.

Fresh Tomato Sauce

This is one good way to use up those little tomatoes that we all have when we grow our own. The sauce can be made up in bulk and freezes well.

1 oz (25 g) butter
2 rashers bacon, chopped
1 large onion, chopped
1 oz (25 g) flour
About ½ pint (300 ml) stock
1 lb (450 g) tomatoes
1 level teaspoon salt
Freshly ground black pepper
A little sugar
1 rounded teaspoon tomato purée
1 bay leaf

Fresh Tomato Soup

Melt the butter in a saucepan and fry the bacon and onion quickly for about 5 minutes, until they are golden brown and the fat has run from the bacon. Stir in the flour and cook for a minute. Add the stock and bring to the boil, stirring.

Roughly chop the tomatoes and add to the sauce with the remaining ingredients, cover the saucepan and simmer gently for 20 to 25 minutes. Sieve the sauce, taste and check seasoning and return the sauce to the pan and reheat. If the sauce seems too thick, add a little extra stock to thin it down.

Gardener's Supper

Make this when courgettes, tomatoes and peppers are at their cheapest in the shops or at their most plentiful in the garden. It is a sort of glorified ratatouille with added courgettes. I like to undercook the vegetables slightly so they remain crisp.

VEGETABLE BASE:

1 tablespoon corn oil
A good knob of butter
8 oz (225 g) onion, chopped
2 cloves garlic, crushed
2 peppers, seeded and chopped
1 lb (450 g) courgettes, sliced
1 lb (450 g) tomatoes, skinned and
  sliced
Salt
Freshly ground black pepper

SAUCE TOPPING:

A good 1½ oz (40 g) butter
1½ oz (40 g) flour
¾ pint (450 ml) milk
1 teaspoon Dijon mustard
Salt and pepper
A little finely grated nutmeg
1 egg, beaten
3 oz (75 g) Cheddar cheese, grated

Measure the oil and butter into a large non-stick pan, then fry the onion gently until tender, increase the heat and stir fry the other vegetables except the tomatoes and season well.

Turn into a large ovenproof shallow dish about 3 pint (1.7 lt) capacity. Top with the tomato slices and season well.

To make the sauce: melt the butter, add the flour and cook for a minute.

Gardener's Supper

Blend in the milk and bring to the boil, stirring continuously until thickened, season well with mustard, salt, pepper and nutmeg.

Remove the pan from the heat, stir in the egg and pour over the vegetables.

Sprinkle with cheese and either brown under a hot grill or put in a hot oven at 400 deg.F, 200 deg.C, gas mark 6 for about 20 minutes.

Serve at once with crusty bread.

Serves 4.

Stilton and Onion Quiche

A very good way of using up the last piece of Stilton. If you have only a little left, make up the weight with other grated cheese.

PASTRY:
6 oz (175 g) plain flour
1½ oz (40 g) lard
1½ oz (40 g) hard margarine
About 2 tablespoons cold water

FILLING:
Knob of butter
4 oz (100 g) onion, chopped
4 oz (100 g) Stilton cheese, crumbled
2 eggs, beaten
½ pint (300 ml) single cream
Freshly ground black pepper
2 oz (50 g) Cheddar cheese, grated
Tomato and parsley for garnish

Heat the oven to 425 deg.F, 220 deg.C, gas mark 7.

Measure the flour into a roomy bowl, add the fats cut in small cubes and rub in with the fingertips until the mixture resembles fine bread-crumbs, add sufficient cold water to mix to a firm dough.

Roll out on a floured surface and line a 9 inch (22.5 cm) flan tin. If time permits, chill the flan for about 20 minutes.

Line the flan with greaseproof paper and baking beans and bake blind for 10 minutes until pastry edges are pale brown. Remove the paper and beans and return to the oven for a further 5 minutes to dry out the centre of the pastry. Reduce the oven temperature to 350 deg.F, 180 deg.C, gas mark 4.

Melt the butter in a small pan and fry the onion until golden brown, then lift out with a slotted spoon and spread over the base of the flan. Sprinkle with Stilton.

Mix the eggs and cream together and season. Pour over the Stilton and onion. Sprinkle with the Cheddar cheese and bake in the oven for about 35 minutes until the flan has set and is a pale golden colour. Garnish with tomato wedges and parsley.

Serves 6.

Stilton and Onion Quiche

Pommes Almandine

This is a rather special way of serving potatoes.

1½ lb (675 g) potatoes
Knob of butter
Salt and pepper
1 egg, beaten
4 oz (100 g) flaked almonds
Deep fat or oil for frying

Cook the potatoes in boiling salted water until tender, drain thoroughly and mash well until smooth. Add a knob of butter and some seasoning and mix well. The mixture needs to be firm, so no milk is added.

With lightly floured hands shape into 12 small croquettes, coat in beaten egg and roll in the almonds, pressing them on firmly. Heat the fat or oil to moderate and fry the croquettes a few at a time over a moderate heat for 3 to 4 minutes until crisp and golden brown. Do not have the fat too hot or the almonds will be dark brown and the potatoes not hot through.

Lift out and drain on kitchen paper and serve piled in a hot dish.

Serves 6.

GAME IN SEASON

All game is seasonal and most of it is strictly preserved. We are aware, thanks to press photographs and gossip columns, that grouse shooting begins on 12th August. The familiar pheasant of our countryside, on the other hand, may not be killed before 1st October. All game must be hung before cooking or freezing, otherwise it would be too tough to eat. The hanging time varies according to taste and is a matter of debate. What some people call well flavoured others describe as rotten. A hare is always a good game buy as there is plenty of meat on it – freeze what you don't need. Venison can work out cheaper than beef. Cook game as you would any other meat. Only tender young birds or animals should be roasted, older ones are good for casseroles, pies and terrines, particularly if marinated first.

Gamekeeper's Venison Pie

Venison is a very lean meat with a delicious flavour. I think it needs to be marinated in wine for a time to make it more succulent and moist.

1½ lb (675 g) stewing venison
½ pint (300 ml) marinade (see basic marinade for game, p. 47)
4 oz (100 g) fatty bacon, cubed
3 oz (75 g) German smoked sausage, skinned and sliced
1 large onion, chopped
Generous 1 oz (25 g) flour
About ½ pint (300 ml) stock
Bouquet garni
1 tablespoon bramble jelly
2 teaspoons salt
Freshly ground black pepper
Dash gravy browning

PASTRY TOPPING:
14 oz (212 g) packet puff pastry, thawed
Egg or milk for glazing

Cut venison into cubes about ¾ inch (1.9 cm) pieces. Marinate in half pint (300 ml) marinade for 24 hours in the refrigerator in a glass or china dish. Lift meat out of marinade, remove and discard any peppercorns, bay leaf, onion and garlic, strain the wine and reserve.

Put the bacon into a non-stick frying pan, cook slowly to draw out the fat then add sliced sausage (if a fat sausage dice it) and onion, cook for about 10 minutes till the bacon is crispy, add flour and blend well.

Make reserved wine marinade up to 1 pint (600 ml) with stock, stir into the pan and bring to the boil, stirring, add venison, bouquet garni and bramble jelly (red currant jelly may be used instead). Season well, add gravy browning, cover and simmer very gently for about 2½ hours until tender. This can be done in a slow oven 325 deg. F, 160 deg. C, gas mark 3, if preferred. Check seasoning. Place a pie funnel or handleless cup in the centre of a 2½ pint (1.4 lt) pie dish, add meat and leave to cool.

Roll out pastry on a floured surface, use to cover the pie. Roll out any trimmings and decorate with leaves made from these. Glaze and bake at 425 deg. F, 220 deg. C, gas mark 7, for about 30 minutes until the meat is piping hot and the pastry golden brown.

Serves 6.

Gamekeeper's Venison Pie

18th Century Pigeons

When I was researching for a good pigeon recipe I found no less than 18 of them in my 18th century book 'The Art of Cooking Made Plain and Easy'. In those days they were plentiful and extremely popular. Most of the recipes start off by stuffing the "belly" with fresh sweet herbs then slow roasting or casseroling them.

4 pigeons, plucked and prepared
4 sprigs fresh thyme
4 sprigs fresh parsley
4 sprigs fresh marjoram
1 tablespoon oil
Large knob butter
4 onions, sliced
4 oz (100 g) button mushrooms
Heaped teaspoon flour
½ pint (300 ml) cider
2 stock cubes, crumbled
Salt
Ground black pepper
A little ground mace or nutmeg
Chopped parsley and thyme to
  garnish

Heat oven to 325 deg.F, 160 deg.C, gas mark 3. First take the pigeons and put a bunch of the 3 herbs inside the carcass. Take a non-stick frying pan, add oil and butter and heat till the butter has melted. Brown birds on all sides, lift out and put to one side.

Add onions and toss in the fat to take up all the sediment, add mushrooms and cook for about a minute, turning. Stir in flour, blend well, then add cider and stock cubes. Bring to the boil and season with salt, pepper and mace or nutmeg. Pour this mixture into a casserole large enough to take the 4 pigeons.

Arrange pigeons on top, season breast of pigeons with salt and pepper. Cover and cook for 2 to 3 hours until the birds are tender. This of course will depend on the age of the pigeons. Check the seasoning of the onion sauce mixture. Sprinkle the birds with chopped parsley and thyme and serve.

This cooking time may seem long for such small birds but very often they do take three hours or even longer.

Serves 4

18th Century Pigeons

Pheasant Normandy

The cooking time will vary with the age of the pheasants. If making this for an occasion, make ahead, then cool and keep in the refrigerator until needed. Reheat until piping hot.

2 tablespoons corn or vegetable oil
Brace of pheasants
2 oz (50 g) bacon finely chopped
1 onion, chopped
1 large clove garlic, crushed
1 lb (450 g) cooking apples, peeled,
  cored and sliced
Heaped tablespoon flour
¾ pint (450 ml) cider
Salt and freshly ground black pepper
Chopped parsley

Heat the oven to 350 deg.F, 180 deg.C, gas mark 4.

Heat one tablespoon oil in a large frying pan and fry the pheasants until lightly browned all over. Lift out and place in the base of a large ovenproof casserole. In the same pan fry the bacon, onion and garlic for about 10 minutes until golden brown. Spoon over the pheasants.

Heat the remaining tablespoon of oil and fry the slices of apple until just tender. Stir in the flour then gradually add the cider, stirring continuously.

Allow the sauce to thicken, pour over the pheasants. Season well. Cover the casserole and cook in oven for 1½ hours or until tender.

Lift the pheasants out of the dish and carve off the leg portions, then carve the breasts and discard the ends of the wings and the carcass (use for soup). Purée all the liquid in a blender or processor. Rinse out the casserole and return the meat to it. Taste and check seasoning and pour the sauce over the pheasant. Reheat in the oven and serve well sprinkled with chopped parsley.

Serves 6 to 8.

Game Pâté

Game Pâté

*Use any game meat you have. I used a
badly shot pheasant for this one plus a
little venison.*

8 oz (225 g) boned raw lean game e.g.
  pheasant, venison roughly cubed
¼ pint (150 ml) basic game marinade
  (page 00)
1 slice bread
8 oz (225 g) belly pork
8 oz (225 g) piece fatty bacon
8 oz (225 g) chicken livers
1 egg
2 teaspoons salt
Ground black pepper
2 cloves garlic, crushed
Scant level teaspoon ground nutmeg
1 tablespoon chopped fresh herbs

FOR TOPPING:
¼ pint (150 ml) aspic if liked
Tomato and cucumber for garnish
First soak the venison in the marinade
overnight. Next day pick out the meat
from the marinade, strain off the wine
liquid and soak the bread in this. Put
the meats, one at a time, through the
processor, taking care not to make
them too fine – except in the case of
the liver which should be a purée.
Alternatively, mince the meats
through a coarse mincer. Add the
squashy soaked bread to one of the
meats when in the processor or
mincer.

  Mix all the prepared meats, remaining marinade, egg, salt, pepper, garlic,
nutmeg and herbs. Mix well, turn
into a buttered 2 pint (1 lt) terrine.

Cover, stand in a roasting tin half
filled with boiling water and cook at
350 deg.F, 180 deg.C, gas mark 4, for
about 2 hours until when pierced with
a fine skewer the juices that run out
are clearish.

  Cool for several hours, then if liked
float aspic jelly over the top. The best
aspic I think comes in packets from
Switzerland or Germany. Garnish
with slices of tomato and cucumber.

Old English Jugged Hare

For this recipe I have not included the blood as I find it often curdles while you are keeping it hot or reheating it, so throw the blood away. A must are savoury forcemeat balls, and serve with red currant jelly.

2 oz (50 g) bacon fat or good dripping
1 hare, jointed
2 onions, coarsely grated
¼ pint (150 ml) inexpensive port
1 tablespoon lemon juice
1 pint (600 ml) stock
4 sticks celery, chopped
2 tablespoons red currant jelly
1 good teaspoon salt
Ground black pepper
Bouquet garni

BEURRE MANIE:
2 oz (50 g) butter
2 oz (50 g) flour

FORCEMEAT BALLS:
2 oz (50 g) bacon, chopped
2 oz (50 g) shredded suet
Grated rind of lemon
2 tablespoons chopped parsley
4 oz (100 g) white breadcrumbs
1 egg, beaten
Salt
Ground black pepper
Little oil and butter for frying

Preheat the oven to 325 deg.F, 160 deg.C, gas mark 3.

Melt the bacon fat or dripping in a large frying pan, fry the hare joints a few at a time, browning on all sides. Arrange them in a large casserole close together. Fry the onions for 5 minutes in sediment remaining in pan, scraping any sediment off the base of the pan and blending in with onions. Turn contents of the pan into a flameproof casserole with the remaining ingredients.

Bring the casserole to the boil on top of the hob, cover with a lid, transfer to the oven and simmer gently for about 3 to 4 hours (depending on the age of the hare), until tender.

Make the beurre manié, cream the butter with the flour. Remove casserole from the oven, lift out the joints on to an enamel plate, discard bouquet garni, add teaspoons of the beurre manié to the hot liquid in the casserole. Heat on top of the hob, stirring until thickened. Taste and check seasoning. If liked the sauce may be strained. Return the meat to the casserole and reheat.

Meanwhile prepare the forcemeat balls. Measure all the ingredients into a bowl, blend well, seasoning with salt and pepper, shape into about 12 balls then fry until crisp and brown on all sides. Add to the jugged hare just before serving.

If liked, serve with fried bread croûtes as well.

Serves 6.

Game Soup

The basis of any good soup is the stock, so for a really good game soup, put bones and carcass in a large saucepan with onion, herbs and seasoning, cover with cold water and bring to the boil. Simmer very gently for an hour, then strain off the stock and if there is any meat on the bones this may be kept to add to the soup.

2 oz (50 g) dripping or bacon fat
2 onions, roughly chopped
2 large carrots, roughly chopped
2 sticks celery, sliced
2 oz (50 g) flour
2½ pints (1.4 lt) good game stock
Salt
Freshly ground black pepper
A little sherry or port (optional)

Melt the dripping or bacon fat in a large saucepan and add the vegetables. Cover and cook gently for 10 minutes. Stir in the flour and cook for 2 to 3 minutes to brown lightly. Blend in the stock and bring the soup to the boil, stirring. Season well and cover and cook gently for about 30 minutes or until the vegetables are cooked.

Remove from the heat and purée in a blender or processor.

Rinse out the saucepan and return the soup to it. Bring to the boil and taste and check seasoning, if liked stir in a little sherry or port before serving.

Serve very hot.

Serves 6 to 8.

Rabbit in Mustard Sauce

Rabbit is often a good buy. The cooking time may be a little shorter or longer depending on the rabbit. If preferred the onions may be strained from the stock, personally I like them in! Serve with a green vegetable such as broccoli.

CASSEROLE:
1 rabbit, jointed
½ pint (300 ml) stock
1 large onion, chopped
Bay leaf
Zest of one lemon
Salt
Freshly ground black pepper

SAUCE:
1 oz (25 g) butter
1 oz (25 g) flour
About ½ pint (300 ml) milk
Scant level tablespoon dry mustard
Scant tablespoon sugar
1 tablespoon vinegar

TO SERVE:
8 fried bread croûtons

Heat the oven to 350 deg.F, 180 deg.C, gas mark 4.

Put the jointed rabbit and other casserole ingredients in the dish and season. Cover and cook in the oven about one hour or until tender. Pierce the rabbit with a skewer to test – it should not fall off the bone.

Lift out the rabbit with a slotted spoon on to a plate, discard the bay leaf. Make the juices and onion up to ¾ pint (450 ml) with milk. Make a roux by melting the butter in a large saucepan and adding the flour, cook for a minute, without colouring. Stir in the milk and stock and bring to the boil, stirring until thickened. Blend the mustard, sugar and vinegar together and add to the sauce. Taste and check seasoning. Return the rabbit to the sauce and heat through.

Rinse out the casserole and use as a serving dish.

Garnish with fried bread croûtons.
Serves 4.

Pressed Game Pie

The pastry used in this recipe is different from the usual shortcrust. It is easy to make and wonderfully crisp.

FILLING:

8 oz (225 g) pork sausage meat
8 oz (225 g) chicken breasts, cut in strips
1 lb (450 g) venison, coarsely minced or processed
8 oz (225 g) fatty bacon, coarsely minced or processed
1 tablespoon chopped fresh mixed herbs
1 teaspoon ground mace
2 teaspoons salt, depending on the saltiness of the bacon
Freshly ground black pepper
6 small hard-boiled eggs, shelled
Beaten egg and milk to glaze

PASTRY:

12 oz (350 g) plain flour
1 teaspoon salt
5 oz (150 g) lard
¼ pint (150 ml) and 2 tablespoons of water

Grease an 8 inch (20 cm) loose bottomed cake tin. Put the sausage meat, chicken, venison, bacon, herbs and seasoning in a bowl and mix thoroughly.

Now make the pastry: put flour and salt in a bowl. Put the lard and water into a pan and allow the lard to melt and the water to boil. Make a well in the centre of the flour and pour on all the liquid, mixing well with a wooden spoon or fork until it becomes a smooth dough.

When cool enough to handle take ⅔ of the dough and slip this into the tin and with the hands work it evenly over the base and up the sides until it stands about 3 inches (7.5 cm) from the base.

Put half the meat mixture in the tin, level and make six dents in the mixture and arrange the eggs in them. Cover with the remaining mixture and flatten.

Brush the inside of the pastry top with beaten egg and milk. Roll out the remaining pastry to a circle just over 8 inches (20 cm) for the lid and lift on to the pie, press the edges firmly together and flute, using the thumb and first finger of the right hand and the index finger of the left hand. Make four holes in the top of the pie and decorate with pastry leaves if liked. Brush with beaten egg and bake in the oven at 425 deg.F, 220 deg.C, gas mark 7, for 45 minutes. Reduce the heat to 350 deg.F, 180 deg.C, gas mark 4 for a further 30 minutes.

Remove from the oven and leave to cool in the tin. Chill the pie overnight before turning out and serving sliced in wedges.

Serves 8 to 10.

Basic Marinade for Game

½ pint (300 ml) red wine
2 bay leaves
8 peppercorns
2 cloves garlic, split in 4
2 tablespoons oil
1 sliced onion

Put all ingredients in a glass or china bowl. Add meat, turn meat in the marinade, cover bowl with a plate, leave in refrigerator for 1 to 2 days (if the meat is cut up small marinate for the shorter time), turn meat frequently. When ready to use lift out meat carefully, discard any peppercorns or garlic sticking to the meat. Strain the wine liquid and use as part of the sauce later.

HOME BAKING

As days shorten and it grows colder outside, a warm kitchen smelling deliciously of home baked bread and cakes is one of the joys of autumn. Sweet or savoury, rich or plain, the products of our own ovens always taste twice as good as those that come off the shelves of a shop. The secret of success is to know your oven. If you are worried about the temperature, it is simple enough to buy an oven thermometer and check it yourself. Have the right equipment – enough baking tins in the sizes you need, mixing bowls and measuring jugs. Unless you have very good non-stick ones, do take time to grease and line your tins with greaseproof paper; it is a pity to make a successful cake and then not be able to get it out of the tin! Before you begin, assemble your ingredients and weigh them out. This saves a lot of time in the long run and makes sure you forget nothing.

Chocolate Orange Sponge

Chocolate and orange make an ideal combination. The orange in the cake helps to give it a moist texture.

3 tablespoons orange juice or the
    juice of half an orange
Grated rind of one orange
3 level tablespoons cocoa
6 oz (175 g) soft margarine
6 oz (175 g) caster sugar
6 oz (175 g) self-raising flour
3 eggs
1½ level teaspoons baking powder

ICING:
3 oz (75 g) soft margarine
8 oz (225 g) icing sugar, sieved
3 tablespoons orange juice or the
    juice of half an orange

Heat the oven to 350 deg.F, 180 deg.C, gas mark 4. Grease and line with greased greaseproof paper two 8 inch (20 cm) round sandwich tins. Heat the orange juice in a small saucepan, with the rind.

Put the cocoa in a large bowl and add the orange juice and blend well. Cool, and add the remaining cake ingredients to the bowl and beat with a wooden spoon for 2 to 3 minutes until the mixture is well blended. Turn into the tins and bake in the oven for 25 to 30 minutes. When cooked the cake will spring back if lightly pressed with the finger. Turn out and remove the paper and leave to cool on a wire rack.

Now make the icing: beat the margarine in a bowl until soft, add the icing sugar and orange juice and beat again until light and fluffy. Sandwich the cakes together with half the icing and put on a plate. Swirl the remaining icing over the top of the cake with a round bladed knife and leave to set.

Hideaway Cake

This is a fun cake, everybody enjoys finding the nuts and small pieces of chocolate in their slice.

4 oz (100 g) soft margarine
4 oz (100 g) soft brown sugar
2 eggs
4 oz (100 g) plain flour
2 oz (50 g) drinking chocolate
1 level teaspoon baking powder
2 oz (50 g) chopped walnuts
2 teaspoons coffee essence or 2
    teaspoons instant coffee dissolved
    in a little hot water
3½ oz (100 g) bar milk chocolate
Icing sugar

Heat the oven to 350 deg.F, 180 deg.C, gas mark 4. Grease and line with greased greaseproof paper the base of an 8 inch (20 cm) cake tin.

Cream the margarine and sugar together. Beat in the eggs one at a time. Sieve the dry ingredients together and fold in with the nuts and coffee.

Cut each square of chocolate into 4 pieces and fold through the cake. Turn into the tin and bake in the oven for 45 minutes.

Turn out, remove the paper and leave to cool on a wire rack.

Sprinkle with icing sugar.

Chocolate Chews

These crunchy fingers are always very popular with children.

5 oz (150 g) margarine
5 oz (150 g) caster sugar
3 oz (75 g) desiccated coconut
5 oz (150 g) self-raising flour
2½ oz (62 g) crushed cornflakes
4 level tablespoons chocolate powder

ICING:
6 oz (175 g) icing sugar
2 level tablespoons chocolate powder
About 4 tablespoons milk

Heat the oven to 350 deg.F, 180 deg.C, gas mark 4. Grease a tin 11 inches by 7 inches (27.5 by 17.5 cm).

Melt the margarine in a saucepan, remove from the heat and stir in all the other ingredients, mixing well. Press evenly into the tin and bake for 30 minutes. Remove from the oven and leave to cool slightly, cut into 16 fingers while still warm.

Sift the icing sugar into a bowl, add the chocolate and blend with just enough milk to make a thick smooth icing. Spread over the fingers, then lift out and leave to set on a wire rack. If necessary trim any rough edges.

Makes 16 chews.

The Castles Chocolate Mocha Cake

This recipe was given to me at the school fête. It is easy and quick, made in a blender or processor.

6½ oz (187 g) self-raising flour
5 oz (150 g) caster sugar
2 eggs
¼ pint (150 ml) oil
¼ pint (150 ml) milk
1 teaspoon bicarbonate of soda
2 tablespoons golden syrup
2 tablespoons cocoa

ICING:
3 oz (75 g) soft margarine
8 oz (225 g) icing sugar, sieved
1 tablespoon milk
1 tablespoon coffee essence
Chocolate flake or grated chocolate

Heat the oven to 325 deg.F, 160 deg.C, gas mark 3. Grease and line two 8 inch (20 cm) sandwich tins with greased greaseproof paper.

Blend all the ingredients together until smooth. Pour into the tins and bake in the oven for 40 minutes or until cake springs back when pressed and comes away from the sides. Cool and then remove the paper.

For the icing: put the margarine, icing sugar, milk and coffee essence in a bowl and beat until smooth. Spread ⅓ of this mixture on to one cake and put the other one on the top. Cover top with remaining icing and mark attractively with a palette knife.

Decorate the top with chocolate flake or grated chocolate.

Basic Fruit Loaf

So easy to make and ideal for cutting a slice for a lunch box.

4 oz (100 g) self-raising flour
3 oz (75 g) light soft brown sugar
3 oz (75 g) soft margarine
2 eggs
2 oz (50 g) glacé cherries, quartered
6 oz (175 g) mixed dried fruit

The Castles Chocolate Mocha Cake

Heat the oven to 300 deg.F, 150 deg.C, gas mark 2. Grease and line with greased greaseproof paper a 1 lb (450 g) loaf tin.

Place all the ingredients in a large roomy bowl and beat well until blended, about 2 minutes.

Turn into the tin and smooth the top. Bake in the oven for 1½ hours or until the cake is a pale golden brown and has shrunk slightly from the sides of the tin. A warm skewer inserted in the centre of the cake will come out clean when the cake is cooked.

Leave to cool in the tin and turn out, remove the paper and store in an airtight tin.

Lancashire Ginger Biscuits

These are quick and easy and sold like hot cakes at the school fête!

12 oz (350 g) self-raising flour
4 oz (100 g) demerara sugar
4 oz (100 g) soft brown sugar
1 teaspoon bicarbonate of soda
3 teaspoons ground ginger
1 egg
4 oz (100 g) butter
1 generous tablespoon golden syrup

Heat the oven to 325 deg.F, 160 deg.C, gas mark 3.

Mix all the dry ingredients together then add the beaten egg, with the butter and syrup which have been melted together, mix thoroughly. Roll into small balls and place on a greased baking tray about 2 inches apart.

Bake in the oven for 20 minutes, they will look like bought ginger nut cookies. Lift off the baking trays and cool on a wire rack.

Makes about 50.

Cakes are available as packet mixtures which can be mixed up and cooked. Many people prefer to spend their time on fancy icings and fillings rather than the basic mixture. For those who still like making the basics, much of the hard work can be done by using electric mixers. Large mixers are necessary for a rich flour and fruit dough.

Lancashire Ginger Biscuits

Harvest Fruit Cake

Harvest Fruit Cake

A very rich moist fruit cake. The fruit is soaked overnight in orange juice and sherry. Do not be generous with the jam or treacle or the cake will sink. This is a shallow fruit cake.

8 oz (225 g) mixed dried fruit
4 stoned prunes, chopped
2 tablespoons sherry
Grated rind and juice of a small
   orange
1 oz (25 g) glacé cherries, quartered
1 oz (25 g) walnuts, chopped
3 oz (75 g) soft butter
2½ oz (65 g) dark soft brown sugar
3 oz (75 g) plain flour
1 level teaspoon mixed spice
2 eggs, blended
A level tablespoon apricot jam
A level tablespoon treacle

TOPPING:
Apricot jam
Glacé cherries
Mixed nuts

Grease and line a 6 inch (15 cm) cake tin with greased greaseproof paper.

The night before, measure the dried fruit and prunes into a saucepan and pour over the sherry and the orange rind and juice. Heat over a moderate heat, stirring for 5 minutes. Cover and leave in a warm place overnight, by then the liquid will be mostly absorbed. Next day add the cherries and nuts to the pan.

Cream the butter and sugar together well. Sieve the flour and spice and add half the flour and blend in, then add the eggs little by little beating well, beat in the jam and treacle. Fold in the remaining flour and fruits.

Turn into the tin and level. Bake in the oven at 275 deg. F, 140 deg. C, gas mark 1 for about 2 hours. Test with a warm skewer, if it comes out clean the cake is done. The top will be paler in colour than usual.

Leave to cool in the tin, then brush with apricot jam and arrange nuts and cherries on top and brush again with jam. Store in a cake tin for up to 3 weeks.

Griddle Pancakes

Very easy to make and ideal to serve to unexpected visitors.

4 oz (100 g) self-raising flour
1 oz (25 g) caster sugar
1 egg
¼ pint (150 ml) milk

Rub the surface of a heavy frying pan or the solid plate of an electric cooker with salt, using a pad of kitchen paper. Grease lightly with lard.

When ready to cook the pancakes, heat the pan or plate until the lard is just hazy, wipe off the surplus with more kitchen paper.

Put the flour and sugar in a bowl and make a well in the centre. Add the egg and half the milk and beat to a thick batter, beat in the remaining milk.

Spoon the mixture on to the heated surface in spoonfuls, spacing well. When bubbles rise to the surface turn over and cook on the other side for about 30 seconds until golden brown. Lift off on to a rack and cover with a clean tea towel.

Continue cooking until all the batter has been used up. Serve fresh and warm with butter and a little homemade jam.

Makes about 18 griddle pancakes.

Griddle Pancakes

Sharp Lemon Tart

This tart has a crisp pastry base with a sharp filling. Nice served cold with whipped cream.

PASTRY:
4 oz (100 g) plain flour
2 oz (50 g) butter
About 4 teaspoons cold water

FILLING:
4 eggs
6 oz (175 g) caster sugar
2 oz (50 g) butter, melted
Grated rind and juice of 2 lemons

Heat the oven to 425 deg.F, 220 deg.C, gas mark 7, with a baking tray placed on a shelf just above the centre.

For the pastry: put the flour in a bowl, add the butter cut in pieces and rub in with the fingertips until the mixture resembles fine breadcrumbs, then add sufficient cold water to mix to a firm dough. Knead lightly until smooth and roll out thinly on a floured surface to line an 8 inch (20 cm) loose bottomed flan tin. Line the flan with a layer of greaseproof paper and baking beans and bake blind on the baking tray for about 12 minutes. Remove the paper and beans and return to the oven for a further 5 minutes to dry out the pastry. Take the flan from the oven and reduce the heat to 350 deg.F, 180 deg.C, gas mark 4.

While the flan is baking make the filling: put all the ingredients except the lemon juice in a bowl and place over a pan of hot water until the butter has melted and the sugar has dissolved, stirring continuously. Stir in the lemon juice.

Pour the filling into the flan and return to the oven to cook for 25 minutes or until the filling has set. Remove and leave to cool, then lift off the flan ring and place on a serving dish.

Serves 6.

Flaky Cheese Crisps

I used to buy wonderful crisp flaky Dutch biscuits, now they are not available locally, so I make my own. They take time but are well worth it. You can freeze the cheese pastry then slice off the biscuits and bake them. Serve them on the day they are made or just reheat them.

1 lb (450 g) plain flour
½ teaspoon dry mustard
1 teaspoon salt
Good pinch cayenne pepper
12 oz (350 g) hard margarine, chilled
About ½ pint (300 ml) water
8 oz (225 g) well flavoured dryish
    Cheddar cheese, coarsely grated

Measure flour, mustard, salt and pepper into a large bowl. Grate the margarine into the flour, using a coarse grater; sprinkle some of the flour over the top of the margarine as it is being grated – this keeps it from sticking. Add the cold water and mix to a dough with a knife.

Flour the table or board, roll out pastry to oblong. Divide the grated cheese into 4 piles. Sprinkle ¾ of the cheese over ⅔ of the pastry, fold in twice again as if you were making flaky pastry, wrap in cling film and chill for 15 minutes or so. Roll out and repeat the process 3 more times. Wrap and chill overnight or for several hours. If time is short freeze for a couple of hours.

Take the block of cheese pastry and cut into ¼ inch slices through the pastry. Lay these strips flat so that you can see the flaky layers. Cut the strips into 1½ inch pieces. Spread out on really well greased baking sheets. Bake at 425 deg.F, 220 deg.C, gas mark 7, for about 10 to 13 minutes until golden brown and crisp.

Makes about 100.

Note: The crisps are inclined to stick during cooking so do grease the trays very well and if liked turn them over with a palette knife just before they are done to finish browning the second side. You could also line the baking trays with silicon non-stick paper and use the same paper for several batches.

IN A NUTSHELL

Hazelnuts, at their plumpest in late autumn, are a familiar part of the country harvest. A few people are lucky enough to have access to walnut trees but walnuts rarely ripen fully in this country and are best used for pickling. All dry nuts store well. Shelled and ground ready to use in recipes, they can be kept in individual bags inside a large bag in the freezer and will still be perfectly good after five years. Nuts are a welcome addition to salads and puddings, invaluable in baking and of course an essential part of a vegetarian diet. And do keep some in a dish with nutcrackers handy so that people can help themselves.

Just Fried Buttered Nuts

Almonds, brazils or cashews are delicious if fried in butter with a little oil and served with drinks.

To each 2 oz (50 g) nuts use
1 oz (25 g) butter
1 teaspoon corn oil

If necessary blanch the nuts to remove the outer skin.

Heat the butter and oil in a frying pan, add the nuts and fry over a moderate heat, turning constantly until golden brown all over. Lift out with a slotted spoon and drain on kitchen paper. If liked sprinkle with a little salt. Turn into a small dish and serve.

Nut Roast

This recipe was given to me by a vegetarian friend. It has a lovely crunchy texture and it also makes a very good stuffing to go with a joint.

4 oz (100 g) ground almonds
4 oz (100 g) hazelnuts, chopped
2 oz (50 g) walnuts, chopped
4 oz (100 g) onions, chopped
8 oz (225 g) cold mashed potato
3 oz (75 g) wholemeal breadcrumbs
2 sticks celery, finely chopped
1 rounded tablespoon chopped
    parsley
1 egg, beaten
Plenty of salt and pepper
3 to 4 tablespoons oil

Heat the oven to 375 deg.F, 190 deg.C, gas mark 5.

Mix all the ingredients together except the oil, seasoning well. Form into a roll and put in an ovenproof dish. Spoon over the oil and bake in the oven for about 45 to 60 minutes, basting occasionally until golden brown and crispy.

Serve with fresh tomato sauce (see page 37) and a green salad or vegetable.

Serves 6.

Mont Blanc

This is a rich special pudding, that is covered in cream to look like a mountain.

8 oz (225 g) dried chestnuts

SPONGE BASE:
2 oz (50 g) caster sugar
2 oz (50 g) soft margarine
2 oz (50 g) self-raising flour
1 egg
½ level teaspoon baking powder

FILLING:
2 tablespoons sugar
4 tablespoons water
2 oz (50 g) soft unsalted butter
½ pint (300 ml) double cream whipped
    until thick
2 to 3 tablespoons sherry

Place the chestnuts in a bowl, cover with cold water and leave to soak overnight.

Heat the oven to 350 deg.F, 180 deg.C, gas mark 4. Grease and flour a one pint (600 ml) pudding basin.

Put all the ingredients for the sponge base in a bowl and beat well until mixed. Turn into the pudding basin and bake in the oven for about 25 to 30 minutes or until risen and golden brown. Remove from the oven, leave to stand for 3 to 4 minutes, then carefully turn out and leave to cool on a wire rack.

While the cake is cooking, drain the chestnuts, place in a saucepan, cover with fresh water and bring to the boil and simmer for about 30 to 40 minutes until tender. Drain and then sieve into a bowl.

Place the sugar and water in a small saucepan and heat gently until the sugar has dissolved, then boil for a minute. Stir into the chestnuts with the soft butter and mix well. Beat in about 3 tablespoons of the whipped cream.

Place the sponge base on a serving dish and pour over the sherry. Pile the chestnut purée on top of the sponge base in a dome and completely cover with cream, using a round ended knife, so that the cream looks like snow on a mountain.

Serves 8.

Hazelnut Meringue

4 egg whites
8 oz (225 g) caster sugar
1½ oz (40 g) ground hazelnuts
About 15 whole skinned hazelnuts
    (optional)

FILLING:
4 oz (100 g) plain chocolate
6 oz (150 g) really soft butter
5 oz (125 g) icing sugar, sieved
4 egg yolks
1½ oz (40 g) ground hazelnuts

TOPPING:
Little sieved icing sugar

Heat the oven to 300 deg.F, 150 deg.C, gas mark 1. Line two large baking sheets with non-stick silicon paper, draw a 7 inch circle on one sheet of paper.

Measure egg whites into a bowl, whisk with an electric whisk or hand rotary whisk until stiff. Then whisk in the caster sugar a teaspoonful at a time on maximum speed, this will take nearly 10 minutes. Fold in ground hazelnuts. Take two teaspoons and make 15 small individual round meringues on the plain sheet of paper, top each with a nut if liked. Spread the remaining meringue to a round on the guide that you have drawn.

Put the large meringue just above centre in the oven and the small ones below. Bake for 1 hour until firm and pale cream coloured, then turn off the heat and leave to cool in the oven for 3 hours.

Make the filling: First, gently melt the chocolate in a bowl over hot water. Cream all the other ingredients together, and finally stir in the chocolate.

Take the large meringue, peel off the paper and carefully lift off and put on a serving plate. Spread the chocolate and hazelnut cream over. Decorate with the small meringues. Do this about 2 to 3 hours before serving.

Serves 8.

Hazelnut Meringue

Buttered Brazils

You can make buttered almonds by the same method

1 oz (25 g) powdered glucose
¼ pint (150 ml) water
8 oz (225 g) granulated sugar
1 oz (25 g) butter
A scant 4 oz (100 g) shelled brazil nuts

Put the glucose, water and sugar in a heavy pan and place on a very low heat until the sugar has completely dissolved; do not allow the mixture to boil.

When the sugar has dissolved, boil the syrup to crack (310 deg.F, 154 deg.C). If you do not have a sugar thermometer, boil the syrup until it is golden brown.

Beat in the butter, then drop in the nuts, making sure that they are well coated with toffee.

Lightly oil a baking sheet and spoon on the nuts. Leave to set.

When set, store in an airtight tin until required.

Praline

This is not difficult to make. Add it to ice cream and special puddings for a different flavour.

1½ oz (40 g) whole blanched almonds
1½ oz (40 g) caster sugar

Put the almonds and sugar in a heavy pan and place over a low heat, stirring occasionally until the sugar has melted, and is starting to caramelise. This will take about 15 minutes.

Continue to cook until the mixture is an even golden brown and the nuts are glazed.

Remove the pan from the heat and pour on to an oiled enamel plate or baking tray.

Leave until quite firm and cold. Turn into a grinder, blender or processor and grind coarsely. Or crush with a rolling pin.

Store in an airtight jar until required.

It is usually better to buy shelled nuts rather than those with the shells still on. It is difficult to tell the quality of the nut by its shell as about half the weight of nuts is shell. There may be even more wastage if the nuts are not in season or of poor quality. To chop nuts use either a sharp knife on a cutting board or a patent nut chopper. To grind you can use an electric blender.

Penn Barn Nutters

So called because I invented these to go with drinks at an exhibition at Penn Barn. If you do not want to pipe the mixture, you could chill it to firm, then roll into 40 small balls.

4 oz (100 g) soft margarine, slightly
    warmed but not melted
2 oz (50 g) semolina
4 oz (100 g) self-raising flour
3 oz (75 g) Gouda cheese, grated
½ level teaspoon salt
½ level teaspoon dry mustard

TOPPING:
40 halved unsalted cashew nuts or 40
    halved blanched almonds

Put all the ingredients except the nuts in a bowl and work together until blended, using a wooden spoon. Take a large piping bag fitted with a ½ inch (1.25 cm) plain icing nozzle. Pipe about 40 small blobs on a large baking sheet. Press a nut in the centre of each.

Bake at 350 deg.F, 180 deg.C, gas mark 4 for about 15 to 20 minutes until a pale golden brown. Cool on a wire rack.

Makes about 40 nutters.

Penn Barn Nutters

Frosted Walnut Cake

*I have happy memories of a Fullers'
walnut cake, and this is very similar.
The icing is far simpler than the
traditional American frosting. By the
way, tartaric acid and cream of tartar
are the same thing.*

THE CAKE:
8 oz (225 g) plain flour
1 oz (25 g) cornflour
3 level teaspoons baking powder
6 oz unsalted butter, softened
12 oz (350 g) caster sugar
Scant 8 fl oz milk
4 egg whites
3 oz (75 g) chopped walnuts

Frosted Walnut Cake

FROSTING:
12 oz (350 g) caster sugar
2 egg whites
4 tablespoons water
½ teaspoon cream of tartar
Pinch of salt
Few drops of vanilla essence

Heat the oven to 350 deg.F, 180
deg.C, gas mark 4. Grease and line
two 8 inch (20 cm) sandwich tins,
using a band of greased greaseproof
paper with a diagonal cut at the base
to fit around the tin. Then drop in a
circle of greased greaseproof paper a
shade smaller than the tin. It is necessary to do this, as the cake rises above
the top of the tin.

Sift flour, cornflour and baking
powder on to a plate. Cream the soft
butter and sugar together until light

and fluffy. Stir in the flour and milk
alternately, with a folding action, until
blended. Whisk the egg whites until
stiff, fold into the cake mixture with
the nuts and divide between the tins.
Bake for about 35 minutes until well
risen. The top will be springy and the
side of the cake shrinking away from
the paper. Cool and remove the paper.

Make the frosting: measure all the
ingredients into a bowl, standing over
simmering water. Stir until the sugar
has dissolved, then whisk with an
electric hand whisk or balloon whisk
until mixture stands up in peaks.
Scrape down the sides of the bowl
from time to time.

Sandwich the cakes together with
a third of the icing and then cover
with the remainder.

Decorate with walnut halves.

Chicken and Chestnut Roulades

These are beaten out breasts of chicken rolled round a chestnut and bacon stuffing. Treble the stuffing recipe and use it at Christmas time for the turkey. Dried chestnuts can be used. Use just 3 oz (75 g), soak overnight, then chop, no need to cook first.

6 chicken breasts

STUFFING:
2 oz (50 g) streaky bacon, chopped
6 oz (175 g) peeled chestnuts, lightly chopped
Small onion, chopped
2 oz (50 g) fresh breadcrumbs
Salt
Ground black pepper
1 egg, beaten

SAUCE:
1 tablespoon oil
Good 1½ oz (40 g) butter
1 small onion, chopped
1½ oz (40 g) flour
¾ pint (450 ml) milk
4 oz (100 g) mushrooms, sliced
3 tablespoons sherry
Salt
Ground black pepper
Freshly chopped parsley

Heat the oven to 350 deg.F, 180 deg.C, gas mark 4.

Beat out the chicken breasts. To do this take a polythene bag and divide into 2 pieces. Sandwich each chicken breast between the polythene and beat with a rolling pin to make a thin fillet like a veal escalope. Repeat with other breasts.

Take a large non-stick frying pan and fry bacon over a low heat till the fat begins to run, then add chestnuts and onion, cover and sauté for about 10 minutes till onion and chestnuts are tender but the nuts still have crunch. Add breadcrumbs, season and bind with egg. Divide stuffing among the chicken breasts, roll up and secure with cocktail sticks.

Heat the oil and half the butter in a frying pan and add the chicken rolls, fry until brown on all sides, lift out with a slotted spoon and remove cocktail sticks. Place in a casserole large enough to take chicken in a single layer. Add the remaining butter to the pan and fry the onion until golden brown, stir in the flour and cook for a minute. Add the milk and bring to the boil, stirring continuously until the sauce has thickened. Remove from the heat. Add the mushrooms to the sauce with the sherry, season well and pour over the chicken. Cook in the oven for about 40 minutes until the chicken is tender. Scatter with parsley.

Serves 6.

Roast Pork with Walnut and Spinach Stuffing

If you have no fresh spinach, use a packet of frozen leaf spinach.

STUFFING:
4 oz (100 g) spinach
1 oz (25 g) butter
1 onion, chopped
2 rashers streaky bacon, chopped
3 oz (75 g) cooked rice
2 oz (50 g) chopped walnuts
1 egg, beaten
Salt and pepper
3 lb (1.3 kg) piece spare rib of pork

Heat the oven to 350 deg.F, 180 deg.C, gas mark 4.

Make the stuffing: wash the spinach, take out any stalks, place in a pan and cook quickly for a minute, until soft and the water has evaporated. Chop well.

Melt the butter in a small saucepan, add the onion and cook for 5 minutes until soft, add the bacon and fry quickly until crisp. Remove from the heat and stir in the remaining stuffing ingredients, mix well.

Stuff the piece of pork, putting any spare stuffing in a small dish. Tie the pork into shape with string.

Roast in the oven for about 2 hours or until the juices run clear. If there is any spare stuffing, put it in the oven for the last 30 minutes of the cooking time.

Serves 8.

Chicken and Pineapple Mayonnaise

Chicken and pineapple make a lovely combination in a salad. The nuts give an added crunch.

3 lb (1.3 kg) cooked chicken
1 small fresh pineapple
½ pint (300 ml) mayonnaise
Juice of half a lemon
Salt
Freshly ground black pepper
Lettuce and watercress
1 oz (25 g) flaked browned almonds

Take the meat from the chicken and cut into neat pieces.

Slice the pineapple and remove the skin and centre core. Cut three slices in half and reserve for garnish, chop the remainder. Chill until required.

Put the mayonnaise and lemon juice in a bowl and mix well, then stir in the chicken. Cover and leave in a cool place until required. When ready to serve, drain any juice from the chopped pineapple, stir into the chicken mayonnaise and mix well. Season to taste.

Arrange a bed of lettuce on a serving dish and spoon the chicken and pineapple into the centre, arrange the six half slices of pineapple around the edge of the dish. Garnish with small sprigs of watercress and sprinkle with the flaked almonds.

Serves 6.

INDEX